A **soulmate** isn't someone who completes you. No, a **soulmate** is someone who inspires you to complete yourself. A soulmate is someone who loves you with so much conviction, and so much heart, that it is nearly impossible to doubt just how capable you are of becoming exactly who you have always wanted to be.

Bianca Sparacino

A Year of Love

Taking Risks, Big and Small
Finding My Soulmate to WIN IT ALL

LISA BREARLEY

First published by Ultimate World Publishing 2023
Copyright © 2023 Lisa Brearley

ISBN

Paperback: 978-1-922982-06-3
Ebook: 978-1-922982-07-0

Cover design: Ultimate World Publishing
Layout and typesetting: Ultimate World Publishing
Editor: Carmela Julian Valencia

Ultimate World Publishing
Diamond Creek,
Victoria Australia 3089
www.writeabook.com.au

Testimonials

Scott has been the BEST thing that ever happened to Lisa. I've known Lisa for over a decade, and I see how Scott's love and partnership have supported my beautiful friend in seeing the woman she was meant to be. Thank you, Scott, for this. I love you and all the things you are doing together with Lisa. It is very inspiring.

Friend, Shalan

From the very first time we met, I knew Lisa came from her heart in everything she thought and did. However, because of that feeling of fear and "I'm not good enough" and that she didn't matter, she was silent. After all those years of uncertainty in herself, she met Scott. Where once Lisa was tightly wound up in her cocoon, Scott supported her in becoming a butterfly!! Now, Lisa exudes confidence, beauty, happiness and has an anything-is-possible attitude. For Lisa, failure is not an option, only a stepping stone.

Friend, Audrey

Some people may be surprised to hear you are writing a book. Not me! You are very good at expressing yourself. I remember when you were young, and you would even make up your own ending to a storybook, which you thought was more suitable to the story. I'm very proud of you and your work and educating yourself and others. I wish you all the best in your writing endeavours.

Mom, Eleanor and Lisa's Kindergarten Teacher

Dedication

This book is written for you. The "you" that deserves a change in your life. The "you" that deserves love in your life. The "you" that knows that love, care and respect are possible. The "you" that knows anything is possible. The "you" that needs someone to believe in you. The "you" that knows life is REALLY about taking a risk. This book is for you.

I have been where you may be right now—in a place of not feeling worthy or deserving, stuck in a place where change seems impossible, a place where I wondered what I really wanted. Was it out there? How could I find it, and how could I keep it?

I have written this book for me and for you.

Contents

Preface

Lisa Brearley, the author of this autobiography, grew up on the North Shore of Prince Edward Island, where the seaside salt air and the whisper of the winds influenced her writing creativity.

In addition to her passion for writing is her passion as an elementary school teacher for twenty years. Throughout her latter teaching years, Lisa decided it was time to pursue a reflection of her own life, through which she discovered her ultimate passion: life, self-identification, self-growth and self-gratification.

During Lisa's journey, she found her true soulmate, best friend and now husband. It was fate that brought them together while walking similar paths. Their individual quest for self-discovery continues to make their love and commitment to themselves and each other stronger than the day before. This book will walk you through Lisa's story of life, love and the pursuit of happiness.

Friend of forty years, Sandra Blacquiere

Introduction

It all started with two souls wanting something better. Myself, a recently divorced (actually, not divorced during most of this "year of love") woman venturing out into her new life. Scott—a man who is also divorced, twenty years sober, a survivor of cancer and manages his diabetes without medication—is also wanting more in his life. We would meet in a place where souls got vulnerable and stories were shared. We were never the same after we met on August 15, 2021.

Join me on my journey. A year with so many learning moments and points of awareness that I would never have seen coming. I look back at pictures and find one of myself in a canoe with my sister Lana on the reservoir in Calgary, Alberta on August 5, 2021. I would never have foreseen the life journey I was about to take on, the strengths I would find in myself that I never knew existed, the courage I never knew was inside me, the brave soul that bared her soul.

This is a chronological recap of my experiences and *Aha!* moments from August 2021 to July 2022—a true blessing of a year I would never trade for anything and daily give gratitude to. A year that was challenging and yet the most rewarding of my life. A year of frustrations, dilemmas, discouragements and points of low; yet a year filled with gratitude, rejoicing, pleasure and so many successes. An understanding that life is the most beautiful when all these emotions can be explored and expressed.

10 Days Before Meeting Scott. With my sister Lana.

This whole personal development journey was first introduced to me by a great friend, Carolyn. I had known Carolyn for several years at this point. She, like me, was going through challenges in her marriage. Having just separated from her husband, she invited me over to her house for a visit on her back deck to catch up on how things were going.

She told me about a three-day weekend course I should consider taking because she saw that I needed some direction in my life. That conversation was where all my growth and own personal development started.

I am grateful for Carolyn. I know now that she only introduced this to me for two reasons: She loved and cared for me enough to suggest it, and she was also in a course herself (which I later attended this year) that promoted "enrolment" into this three-day personal development course.

I took the three-day course in person, just before Covid hit the ground running in February 2020. It was very eye-opening. I made discoveries about myself and took away tools I still use today. I'm so grateful and blessed for that experience.

I am truly grateful to Carolyn and forever will thank her and do it publicly in this book.

Thank you so much, Carolyn

As of August 15, 2021, I have been separated from my husband of twenty-six years. I had decided a year earlier and found some sense of bravery. I didn't tell him I needed a divorce; however, I thought about my words carefully. I had just come back from a walk with my Great Pyrenees dog, Alya, and sat down on the back deck of our house in Calgary. My former husband was enjoying a beer, and I found that ounce of brevity and spilled out a simple sentence. I could not believe this was coming out of my mouth. I said, "I need to move on."

I don't remember what else I said. All I remember was that I didn't need some big fight back, so I did not say, "I want a divorce."

I was at a point in my life where I needed to have simple clarity. He needed no explanation, no long-winded *blah-blah-blah*. It just needed to be simple. I may have even said, "I need to move on for me." That's it. Seven words that were not arguable, not disputable. I thought they were clear and precise.

At that point, I felt a big relief—HUGE. I was making a decision. Me! I was making a decision and sticking to that decision.

Yes, it seems like it may not be a risk to anyone else to state your feelings. However, stating what I wanted and needed was a HUGE thing for me. I feel like I haven't really been heard or seen in most of my life. I had lost Lisa in the forty-eight years of my life.

My two older siblings, Lana and Darren, are smart and have paved their own paths. As the third child, I was to do what was right and learn from any bumps they experienced. You see, I grew up in a great Catholic family where doing and showing "goodness" was a common way of being. Going to church, being a great contributor to the community, having a well-kept, lovely home, doing your best in school and so on. There was no real room for mistakes.

Introduction

I married early at twenty-two, with all great intentions of staying married and having children. I had two beautiful children by the age of thirty. I would never change bringing those two beautiful souls into the world. However, at thirty I was losing an understanding of who I was. Children were a priority, and I got lost in that priority.

I slowly started to see my potential when I began to prioritize my health and emotional growth in 2019. I did not fully realize that if I worked on my physical and emotional health, I could show up to life with more me, which meant healthier relationships and bringing more to the table. I also knew I wasn't too old to make a change in my life. No matter my age, I could start over and things could improve.

So here I was in 2020, telling my former husband I needed to move on for myself. Fast forward to July 1, 2021: We had just sold our family home, and I bought *my* first home where my 18-year-old daughter, Brianna, and I moved into.

I was proud of my new home. It was everything I was looking for. Hardwood floors, great community, fenced-in yard for my eighty-pound Alya, a garage and only four steps up to the bathroom and bedrooms.

All of July, I enjoyed organizing my house how I wanted it, purchasing Marketplace items to decorate and buying some new items off Amazon. I was making decisions!

Brianna and I took on a DIY project. I researched floor coverings, and we went on a search for a colour and style we liked and a price I could budget for. Then, we got to work and laid down the laminate click flooring in Brianna's basement room. We worked together as a team, and I think we rocked it! I loved doing this project with her!

Brianna and I installing floor

I spent this month and the next connecting with my sister, Lana, as she and I were in the same boat—divorced and recently in our own homes. I was excited for my "new life" and was looking forward to spending more time with Lana, as my new house was now closer to hers.

I also looked forward to paying bills. Can you believe I never learned how to really be in charge of paying bills? My former husband did all of that. So, I had a lot of learning to do. I am still learning over a year later.

I made myself take on a small mortgage to learn to budget and be responsible for paying a bill. I know it sounds a little odd. However, I needed this responsibility because dealing with finances was (and can still be) a daunting thing for me. I also continue to learn about money and improve my relationship with it.

During July and August, I enjoyed quiet time in my home—a space with few interruptions. It was a time to be with only myself, have some much-needed therapy with my dog, and attempt to have more meaningful time with my daughter. I made a choice of a new car for myself too. A Toyota Rav4—my first car—known for lasting a long time and being reliable. I made a great choice—a choice and decision that I had never really made before.

I felt great making decisions and feeling confident about my choices. I did not need a man; I was doing great.

I was excited about an upcoming retreat I was about to attend and looked forward to the possible chance to grow and learn. This retreat was the next step in the progression of the personal development courses. At this point, I was excited about opening a richer connection with my daughter and my son, Jordan, who at that point lived with his father.

As a teacher, and not working during July and August, it meant I could focus on myself and not be distracted. I was excited for my week of personal growth coming up in mid-August. Shortly after, it's back to work and teaching Grades 1 and 2.

I was ready to grow. I was ready, and I was so damn scared too.

CHAPTER 1

August 2021

The Risk

With all the changes over the last few years around Covid guidelines and protocol, I found myself attending the same personal development course as Scott, which was held at The Eagles Nest Ranch in Medicine Hat, Alberta, Canada. The original location, before Covid threw a wrench in everything, was in California, United States. However, with all the restrictions and such, a new Canadian location was established. Ironically, we both signed up for this course at this location. Who knew the universe would find its way for us to meet?

Taking this week-long course was also a sign to me that making an investment in myself was something new I was choosing. For most of my life, I desired very little and often felt guilty about spending money on what I really needed or wanted. It wasn't until the latter part of my first marriage that I started to shift towards spending money on my health and well-being. This was one of those choices for me. Costing under ten thousand dollars, I knew I would experience something I'd never experienced before this week-long course.

The company I was taking this personal development course from has been around for almost fifty years, and testimonials from others were only positive. I knew I had nothing to lose. Little did I really know how this seven-day course would shift my life.

Scott's experience of the three-day personal development course was a little different than my experience of it back in 2020. When he had originally taken the initial three-day course, the presenter finished with the up-sale to the next course. As Scott says, he wasn't really into his three-day weekend. At that time, he was in a state of frustration and not in a good space, having just gone through surgery for cancer. He said he didn't really benefit from the weekend because his emotional state and openness for growth were very narrow. They were up-selling him, and he walked out to his Harley, was about to raise his leg over to get on it and thought, *I will easily put $5,000 into my bike but will not put it into myself.*

He often retells this story with the fact that he stopped getting on his bike, walked back inside, and bought the seven-day course to the Ranch.

This personal development week at the Ranch in Medicine Hat was a three-hour drive for me from Calgary, Alberta and a ten-hour drive for Scott from Ashcroft, British Columbia. We both began this journey of improving ourselves a few years previous with the three-day weekend course, and this course was the next in the progression of courses.

Most attendees did not know each other prior to the Ranch. Scott and I were not only from two different provinces in Canada, but we also attended two different three-day courses. His course was in Vancouver, British Columbia, and mine was in Calgary. I believe the timing of it all was meant to be. Some things in life are unexplainable; when things happen, they were meant to happen when they were meant to happen.

The time at the Ranch was a time to focus on finding out more about ourselves and who we are and how we show up in this world. With no disruptions, like cell phones, I entered this course with a mindset to work on myself and my relationship with my two grown children—at that point ages eighteen and twenty-three.

I was just a month and a half out of my family home. I purchased my first house and was in my year of separation from my former husband. My goal on this week-long course was to grow and heal, so I could be stronger for myself and thus be more present for my daughter and son.

During that week, I experienced something rather unfamiliar. We were in a forum wherein the more open and honest you were and the more you shared, the more you gained. This is all new for me—coming from a life where everything looked just fine, and I always had a smile on my face. Although hesitant to speak as much as I should, I took, more than typical, opportunities to speak my mind. I remember sharing my worries and fears of not feeling worthy, interesting or smart and how they all kept me in a cage of self-doubt as a woman, mother, partner and teacher.

That week at the Ranch was meant for me. It was a week of growth and to spark a light in my relationship with my daughter and son. After years of feeling challenged with really connecting with my daughter, I knew this would be extremely important for maintaining and improving my connection with my kids. It opened my eyes to what I was capable of. I could see sparks of confidence and worthiness. I could start to see that others saw that in me too. This awareness is something I have not seen (or have rarely seen) during my forty-eight years of life.

The week-long course provided a safe space to see what greatness I had and what I still need to work on or see in myself. I knew I was a loving, caring, patient person. However, I had so much doubt about my worthiness and self-assurance, wondering why anyone would want to be with me.

It was a turning point in my life, and I (again) am so grateful for this experience. I would not change it for anything, as it inspired me in several ways. I had very few real friends whom I connected with regularly, and I knew I would gain a new cohort of friends, or at least others who were also interested in personal growth and moving forward, during this course. True enough, I connected with great people, like Audrey, Julie and Shalan, to name a few, and have kept in contact with them over the past year as I continued to work on seeing the value I bring to friendships.

In the first few hours of this week-long course, we had a short introduction (sit and listen) to what the week would look like and the bare bones of what we needed to know. Then, there was really no holding back at that point. We were asked to step out of our comfort zones and share on many occasions—share as much as possible, so we could learn that being uncomfortable was a time for growth and move forward through it.

As I said, the more you shared, the more you gained in this course. However, I was vibrating with fear and uncertainty. At that point, I lacked confidence in my ability to share so others would understand (as I always thought of it, sounding smart or speaking somewhat eloquently).

Yes, I know I am a teacher, and the act of standing up in front of a bunch of people should come easy to me, but it does not. I can speak in front of three hundred kids. However, baring my thoughts, my soul and my challenges are not only a brand-new venue for me but doing it in front of a bunch of adults also scares the shit out of me.

Scott, on the other hand, seemed to have no fear of sharing, no doubt in his ability to be vulnerable, no worries about what others thought. This was very intriguing and inspiring to me (and as the week went on, I learned he had this effect on others too).

My first chance to step out of my comfort zone was during the first day. It was already a long day, and we were asked to share about ourselves. I don't exactly remember what I talked about—maybe my pity story of not feeling worthy or lacking confidence or my earliest memory of not feeling trusted to help my dad paint the white fence. Either way, the feedback from the facilitator was definitely a stab in my heart (maybe with a little twist—okay, I might be being dramatic. However, that's how I took it!).

"How's that working for you?" asked Cathy, the facilitator.

At that moment, I felt I was reduced to a small ant. I felt like I had no backbone. I felt like I had no legs to stand on. Later, I reflected on that moment and questioned myself, *Why do I feel like this when someone who seems intimidating asks me such questions? Why do I cower?*

To this day, I thank Cathy for bringing me some clarity. I realized that one of my goals in life was to gain more confidence in myself. That I was not the stories I made up about myself and that I was there to kind of "reinvent" Lisa, to bring forth a more confident Lisa. I'm so glad I took a risk on that day. For you, that may seem small. However, the baby steps I took along the way were monumental in moving forward.

One of the first things that was apparent during this course was that I needed to be honest with myself. An exercise that we were asked to do was make a list of qualities we were seeking in a relationship. I knew what qualities I did not want (that seemed for sure).

The moment after making it, I discovered that this list of what I desired and deserved in a relationship was sitting right in front of me. For some reason, and to this day, it was a bit like an epiphany. I felt like the list of my requirements was sitting right in front of me. I read and reread the list. I looked at Scott and looked at my list. That was when I first thought this list was Scott. I knew, however, I still had to stay focussed on my journey and allow him to focus on his. I was not ready to alter my journey or his for a relationship that (at that point) was uncertain.

I made my list and, as I reviewed it, soon realized that this man, who shared in our group a few times at this point and whose (from what I could see) disposition in life was a picture of someone crying out to be heard, was the list. This "right" partner (on my list) was to possess the ability to share, be authentic, be hardworking, be thoughtful, be independent, have a positive outlook on life and be willing to solve problems.

I had to narrow it down to my top three: sharing, authentic and thoughtful. I knew quite well, at that point, what I did not want in my life. I had ended a marriage where I was not doing well. Communication had to be key in my next relationship. I needed and was looking for a partner who wanted more and better for themselves, who's open to look at themselves or at the least talk openly about their challenges. With that came my interest in Scott. The list I had made about what I wanted in a relationship was Scott. There he was, sitting right there.

On other days at the Ranch, I took more risks, and my confidence level started to feel a little more even-keeled. This came up when we had to sort ourselves by how much money we made. The reason I bring up this activity is because it is a reminder that I should never judge a book by its cover. I was confident walking in there because of the job I held and how much money I made. When we sorted ourselves by the income we earned, I was intrigued that Scott, whose appearance was quite rugged and rough with his tattooed sleeve arms, had an income more than mine. I was interested in knowing more about this—not because I was any sort of gold-digger, that's for sure. On the contrary, not only did he appear to cover all the areas on my list of requirements for a partner, but he was a financially stable man too.

The week went on, and Scott and I enjoyed lunches and dinners together at a common table with other attendees on many occasions— not truly seeking each other out, but I believe we understood that being in each other' presence was safe and enjoyable. There were many occasions throughout the week when we would see and invite the other for lunch or dinner. On a few occasions, we sat only with each other. I looked into those blue eyes with much interest and was excited to get to know this man.

I found myself being aware of his presence in the room during activities and wondering why he would make certain choices. For instance, there was an event that was physically demanding. To not jeopardize their own health or the success of the group activity, he and several others opted out of it. I found myself wanting to know more and learning more about him and his life story.

There were many moments during that week that I questioned myself: What are you doing? Why are you continuing to think about this man? You just separated from your husband of twenty-five-plus years! You will look like you are just jumping onto the next guy you see!

You must be desperate in some manner, not taking the time to grow and learn on your own. What will my family think? My daughter? How will it look? Is it just purely a desire thing? Am I just needing love? Why am I not just happy with myself?

So many questions, yet my gut was telling me differently.

The last time I listened to my gut, I told my husband I needed to move on from our marriage, and I was certain about that "gut feeling." Was my heightened emotional state causing me to not think properly?

I had a lot of self-doubt and a hard time thinking about what I really wanted in life. I needed this journey of personal development to give me some direction on the answers I was looking for.

It wasn't until the last evening, a fun celebration of dinner and dancing, that the two of us better understood that there was an attraction. I was flirting (in that butterfly-printed dress) and was more interested in making a move now that the week was coming to an end.

I felt like it was up to me to make a move. It was time to listen to my gut. I could not let this one go without doing something. I remember putting my mask (Yes, I had a mask for Covid. However, we never had to wear one all week.) in the pocket of his coat, which was hanging on the coat rack, as a memento to remember me by. I didn't know where this relationship was going or if I would ever see him again. However, that never got noticed, and in the end, it was unimportant.

Scott and I both thought the course ended on Sunday. However, it ended on Saturday, and I was not expected to return to Calgary until Sunday. So, we decided to go out for dinner in Medicine Hat (a 45-minute drive from the Ranch). Although, Scott tells the story that he asked me out for dinner, and yes, I think he exclaimed, "So I guess we're going out for dinner!" if I recall.

We travelled in our own vehicles, my small SUV following him behind his big white pickup. I took a picture of his truck when we were stopped at a red light and thought, *Nice ass* (as his was a dually with four tires on the back—ha ha!). *Should I take a picture of this guy's licence? I don't really know him.*

I felt very comfortable and safe around Scott—although nervous, as I had not really *been* in a relationship other than my husband of more than twenty-five years; before that, I was a teenager. So, having this *date* (or you might call it a one-night stand) and taking the initiative to be with a man was a crazy idea for me.

Scott's dually truck and my SUV

We arrived in Medicine Hat, and the chemistry was definitely there. The attraction was there. The need to be together was there. We pulled over in a parking lot, and I got out of my car and hopped into his big, white truck. All I wanted to do was kiss him, hold him, touch him. I felt such a strong connection with him.

This guy was really special. I could not really put into words why I needed to be with him, why I was so attracted to and intrigued by this man. We kissed, which was a bit awkward for me, as kissing someone so passionately was not something I'd done (in a very long time). I think before any words came out, we knew we were not just having dinner. We needed more time together.

As we sat in his truck, we agreed we would get a hotel. I knew I wanted to spend more time with him. I knew I needed to take this risk in my life. You know how you should listen to your gut? Well, my gut was screaming to spend more time with him. I was certain, comfortable and respected in his presence.

There were not too many choices of hotel rooms, and we got a crappy motel room. However, that didn't make a difference because all I knew was that I would spend the night with this man. With my new sense of confidence yet habitual sense of shyness, I must have said many times that this is usually not me; I don't just pick up guys and spend a night in a hotel room. Or maybe that's the tape that played in my head (over and over and over again).

We went to the motel room first. He easily paid for the room, and I (fairly) easily accepted. I thought I would equal out the cost of the hotel room by getting dinner later. Upon entering, I was feeling a little nervous. However, I was completely respected by this new man I hardly knew.

I soon learned of his incontinence (as he had battled and survived prostate cancer and had a radical prostatectomy surgery three years previous). Whereas I was conscious about wearing pantyliners, not knowing when my fibroids or monthly friend would come (pushing forty-nine years old). Nevertheless, we were supportive of each other's "shortcomings" and open to giving each other respect and a sense of comfort as much as possible.

I also had grown into my own body over the years, and the stretch marks I received from having two kids were still something I was unsure about how they made me a sexy woman. I laughed them off and said they were my *tiger marks*—as if I had won some fight. I knew I had a sexy body; however, I was still self-conscious about my behind, always thinking it was a little big. My brother once joked to me to ease my mind (like thirty-five years ago) that it's more cushion for the pushin'. This little piece of advice from him kept me going for many years.

Scott was so gentle yet excited to please me. In many ways, I was turned on by his masculine body and the way he took care of my feminine body. He treated me with such a gentle nature yet turned me on with such passion. As we learned more about each other, I realized I love how Scott had little to no embarrassment about the human body. Feeling a little uncertain about my own body, I saw how he had many scars on his. Throughout the past week, I had never heard about them. However, he was quick to tell me about the many scars on his head, which were a little more obvious.

We were accepting of each other's bodies right away. Why wouldn't we be? There was no need (at our mature ages of forty-eight and fifty-four) to look at superficial marks that make up our past stories. Although, at that point I knew we still had so much to learn from each other. I knew from then that I had so much to learn from him.

This level of comfort with his own body and this level of vulnerability was something I wanted in my partner. Our first night together was very telling of the sexual partner I was also wanting.

Our time in the room was almost like a fantasy to me. A world of care, respect, attention and desire—something I didn't feel for a long time. I've never felt so comfortable (and so attracted and certain) with a man I had just met. I had no worries about him respecting me and that I would be cared for.

He was respectful and loving and possessed passion and desire right from the get-go. Even though this (a one-night stand) was something I had never done before, I've never felt so loved and respected. I felt like this would not be a one-night stand. And then we went to dinner. (And yes, I paid, as I said I would!)

After the hotel, dinner and driving back to Calgary the next day, we stopped in my community's parking lot (in Calgary) to say goodbye (for now). Saying goodbye a week after we met was hard. I did not want him to go.

Then, Scott was back in Calgary within a few days of our first evening together. This gesture blew me away—a man I had just met drove back seven hours after seven hours just a day before to come back to see me. This guy is amazing! As I learned, driving (or riding) is not a big deal to him. However, the reason and purpose of coming back to see me in Calgary so quickly after just meeting was an immense gesture.

In Calgary, after our first night together.

A Little Closer

When Scott returned to Calgary a few days after our hotel and dinner rendezvous, we attended a relationship workshop given by one of the presenters who facilitated the Personal Development course we were just on for the week.

During the evening of this relationship workshop, we sat close (like a brother and sister) yet kept our "relationship" a little hush-hush due to the no-relationship-within-thirty-days policy we were expected to follow after the seven-day course. We learned a lot that evening, and as I sat beside him, I yearned to share and show how much I cared for him. He learned about how he, still being an important part of my life as a partner, was not my priority and that my children always come first. This was a great understanding and very true; however, I also understand that my children are adults and must learn to fail and succeed on their own. The area of children has been a learning curve for us as we spent more time together learning about each other.

We later heard from Cameron, a friend who attended the seven-day course on the Ranch with us, that his wife, who had noticed us sitting beside each other during the relationship workshop, had commented to her husband that we looked like a happily married couple. Very interesting how others see you when the vibes and positive feelings of care and respect are there. I believe Scott and I possessed such positive energy and attraction despite never publicly showing our affection that evening. Cameron's wife did not even know us and only later heard about us after she made that comment to him.

As our understanding that only geographical space seemed to keep us apart, it was time to make plans to book some plane trips. Scott lived in Ashcroft, a three-hour drive to Vancouver, where he would drive weekly (to and back) for work. I would fly into Abbotsford, B.C. or Vancouver every other weekend to see Scott, and he would come to Calgary. I always looked forward to our weekends together. When I arrived in Abbotsford, we often drove back to Ashcroft and other times treated ourselves to a hotel. After several flights back and forth and having to say goodbye for weeks or two in between, Scott had given me a keychain that said, "I love you. One day we will never have to say goodbye, only goodnight" to remind me that flying back and forth would not last forever.

We managed to sort through the flights back and forth. We enjoyed every time we were together. We got to know each other more and more. We did some "normal" things together, like grocery shopping and organizing his house. We also spent a lot of time getting to know each other on an intimate level. We both desired each other and loved exploring and accepting each other's bodies. We truly loved holding, touching and having each other in each other's arms. We loved making sure we were physically together as often as we could be.

Before moving on from August, the month we met, I want to share one very important gift that Scott received during our week at the Ranch. As I mentioned before, I truly admire Scott's ability to hold an audience and capture a feeling in a memory. He often proudly retells this story and enjoys helping others in their relationship with this gold nugget he learned during one of our activities on the Ranch. The exercise we had done required us to think of what we wanted more of in our life.

When Scott was asked this question, he replied that he wanted a partner, a relationship. He wanted to share his life with someone. So, Philipe, one of the several senior personal development staff members, required more from Scott. Philipe asked, "What will you ask her every morning when you wake up?"

Scott said (like many, I'm sure), "Good morning, honey. I love you."

Philipe planted a new seed in Scott's head, which has been a cornerstone for our relationship since we have been together. Philipe said, "Why don't you ask her, 'How can I love you today?'"

Scott reaffirmed that this was an amazing idea.

Well, we do this every morning with each other. Some days are heartfelt answers, like "I just need longer hugs today" or "I need you to be patient with me today." Other days might be, "I need you to connect with your daughter or reach out to a friend." And at the end of the night, in bed, we ask each other, "Did I love you today?" Sometimes it's an easy yes. Other times it's a longer explanation, like "Yes, you loved me when you sent me an email about how you were feeling" or "No, you did not reach out to your friend today as I asked."

We all learn these little nuggets in life, which we both feel was a great one. Thank you, Philipe. This little golden nugget allows us to close any questions or concerns from the day and feel calm and connected going to sleep.

The months to follow August were riddled with a lot of learning, being open for communication and finding ways to make sure we both understand and respect each other in our growth. We had both just been through our own personal work and are now learning about each other. What a journey we would go on over the next eleven months before our wedding on July 23, 2022.

CHAPTER 2

September 2021

My First Ride

On our many rides to and from airports, I learned what kind of music Scott liked. We mostly played his music because he was driving and his phone was connected to Bluetooth in his big-ass truck. His selection varied greatly, something I enjoyed for sure. He liked rock from AC/DC to country rap, such as Colt Ford, to some of the oldies such as one of his favourites, Johnny Cash. Scott enjoyed singing along to many of the singer's tunes, and I enjoyed his love for this. He loved having fun with music, and I loved being in this space when it happened and sometimes singing along with him.

You know, you truly come to appreciate the little things like this. It would put a big smile on my face. I still love when Scott sings to music. I love how Scott loves music and loves to groove and sing too (even though he claims he's not very good at singing along). I love this carefree spirit—something I value and enjoy myself. I get to be free and express myself too (and I do!). I love music and moving to it too.

With our geographical distance, there was no problem keeping in contact daily. We realized we preferred video chat, as seeing each other's face was the most rewarding and kept our conversations more viable. The only challenge was always having enough data (usually on my end—limited data plan!). When I returned to work in September, I called Scott on Facebook Messenger or Facetime every lunch hour. This video connection was important and talking to him kept me grounded and reminded me that I was loved and respected and that I had a partner who cared about my day and wanted to keep connected. Scott has really taught me so much about improving my communication and that showing love is a priority.

As a teacher, I promoted writing in our gratitude journals at least a few times a week. Through this personal development work and since meeting Scott, I've found myself feeling rich with gratitude and wrote about it in my own journal. With my Grades 1 and 2 students, I often wrote about how grateful I was to have Scott in my life and shared it with them. I could tell they appreciated seeing my face light up and hearing about the things we did, like going for rides on his motorcycle. I often took pics of these written gratitude journal entries and sent the pics to Scott. I wanted him to know I was speaking and sharing about us with anyone I knew, as I was so proud and excited to be part of this man's life. He brought such joy and love into my life, and I glowed so much when I spoke of him. This air of love radiated from me when I spoke of him and our relationship with my co-workers at school.

I remember when I returned to work at Earl Grey Elementary School at the end of August 2021. It was tradition to give teachers time to share how their summer went and what they were up to. Well, I'm sure my smile and glowing disposition entered the room before the words came out of my mouth. When it was my turn to share, I talked about the week-long course I was on and how I met Scott that week.

I spoke of how he brought such love and joy to my life and that we are eager to make this work even with the long distance between us. I spoke (and beamed) about how he was such a bright light in my life, and I know other friends and staff at work were happy for me. Many commented how they loved seeing me in this light. They all knew I was doing well with moving on from my previous marriage and were so thrilled to see I was certain about this man and he was certain about me. Some friends already saw Facebook posts or heard through the grapevine about the "new" man in my life, and they were genuinely thrilled for me.

From early on in meeting Scott, I learned about his many accidents, including the first one where he was hit by a car and dragged for many feet when he was seven years old. It took him months to recover. This altered his learning and interest in school. He talked about (and I've witnessed) his challenges with spelling and constructing written work. Despite the lack of attention to spelling or grammatical detail, Scott still possessed a big heart with big emotions and always made sure he got his feelings across to me. On many occasions, he wrote emails to me that just took my breath away. His words were so heartfelt and emotionally driven. Each email he sent made me yearn for him, and I found myself (a teacher for almost twenty years) speechless and unable to equal the emotional level that he wrote. I admired his passion and romantic gestures, another quality I valued in this incredible man.

Scott got my attention one weekend when I went to Ashcroft to see him. He took me on his motorcycle for a ride. Wow! What an experience—exhilarating and scary at the same time. The only way

I could stay on was to hold tight, which of course, I didn't mind. It was late September or early October, and it was a little brisk to be out riding in the mountains. I'm still learning the terminology and catching myself—it's *riding*, not *driving* the motorcycle. The ride on the green Harley Davidson Dyna was a rush. He has been riding for about thirty-plus years and calls it his freedom.

When Scott later brought this bike to Calgary, my daughter was given a ride on the back. It was hard to tell what she thought of the whole new situation; however, my mind raced. Maybe she thought, *How did Mom find this guy, and what does he see in her?* Either way, Brianna and I believe we both have a bit of a fascination with bikes and speed.

Brianna's first-time riding with Scott

Meeting the Family

Shortly after that relationship course we attended, Scott asked me if I was 100 percent committed to us. Without hesitation, I said yes. I (we) took any doubt off the table and were ready to commit to each other.

Did I know exactly what that would look like or how I would make sure I held my end of the commitment? No. All I knew at that point was that the connection I had with this man was something I had not experienced before. It was powerful, and he showed me daily what I wanted in a relationship: A man who was genuine, open, honest, loving, caring, kind and down to earth. He was showing up as a man I connected with without saying words but through how we looked at each other, how we touched each other and through our efforts, such as emails or phone calls. I knew I had no problem committing 100 percent to him and to love.

Within a month of knowing Scott, I wanted to share him with my family. He was an impactful soul that entered my life, and I wanted my family to meet this amazing man.

Ever since Covid started in March 2020, my family decided that it was important to connect with each other on a more regular basis. We decided to Skype call every Sunday, which seemed like a challenge. You see, we were mostly in different parts of the world. My sister and I were in Calgary (Mountain Time), my younger brother Dean was near Toronto (Eastern Time), our parents a three-hour difference from Calgary (Atlantic Time), and my older brother was almost a full day ahead in England (Greenwich Time). However, we made it work. Since our parents are divorced, we decided to give Mom and Dad their own time and not make it uncomfortable for them to be on the same video together.

Well, my siblings and I Skyped one Sunday, and I told them that Scott would be joining us. Lana had already met Scott; Scott and I had gone out for lunch with her. She seemed pretty comfortable with him and happy with my choice (of a new man).

During our lunch date with Lana, Scott expressed to her that he doesn't like how I say sorry a lot. I did say this a lot, and I knew it was a word that confirmed my doubts about my capabilities. I knew that Scott's intention to support me in eliminating my overuse of the word *sorry* was to remind me that what I had to say was important and that I should not have any self-doubt. I started to curb blurting out that word, which made a big shift in what came out of my mouth. Anyway, Lana suggested a *sorry* jar might help curb the number of times I say sorry. I would have to put money into a jar every time I said that word.

Now on one of the first family Skype calls with Scott, Lana was interested in hearing how the *sorry* jar was going. Scott, in his ever-so-wittiness and smart comebacks, said, "Well, Lana, you see, I thought I would bring it up a notch and smack her ass whenever she said sorry. Little did I think she would like getting her ass smacked!"

Well, well, well, well. After that comment, the reactions from my family varied greatly. Lana appeared to not know how to react and didn't say much at all. Dean appeared to think it was funny but a little awkward at the same time. Darren appeared to want to laugh his ass off so hard but wasn't sure if he should. And I believe my mom thought, *I kind of like this guy because I see he makes my daughter very happy.*

The *sorry* jar was never truly operational, and getting my ass slapped was more fun anyway.

Anyways, that was one of Scott's first meetings with my family. That week was Mom's week, which meant Dad was not privy to the *sorry* jar conversation, and that was probably best. Not sure how the slapping-my-ass comment would have impacted my Dad as a first impression of this man I had just met.

CHAPTER 3

October 2021

Fight or Not?

It wasn't always bouquets of roses as many may have thought our relationship was. We had our own bumps in the road and stumbled along the way. We had challenges that, for either of us, could be considered large or small.

Scott thought we were having our first fight over a Facebook post that was about getting the Covid vaccine shot. Scott commented that being forced to get a Covid vaccine shot was like rape because something was being put in his body without his permission.

I learned that Scott did not trust the vaccine shot or that the government was "forcing" us to get the shots, which was affecting him because we needed vaccine shots to travel on a plane to see each other. He often told that story with the fact that he would probably end up in jail if someone told him he could not get on a plane to see his girlfriend. However, this testy subject was in connection to our "first fight."

In one of our daily lunch phone calls, I mentioned that I would like to speak to him about this comment he made on Facebook and how it made me feel uncomfortable, especially using the word *rape* so flippantly. However, I had to get back to work and couldn't continue the conversation at that moment. He said he fretted all afternoon, seeming like it would be a big blow-up and I was all angry with him.

When we connected again after work, I shared with him about my connection to the word *rape* and he saw where I was coming from. We soon started to understand that communication was key, even if we didn't have a solution to what looked like a difference of opinion. And that was the end of our "first fight."

No, it was not a fight. It was one of those first awarenesses in our relationship that we often automatically return to old stories and assume that if an event happens, a familiar consequence will automatically follow this. We were learning a new way to be in a relationship, and this felt so good.

We knew we would not always see eye to eye and have the same opinions, and that was okay. We've come up against this wall on many occasions where our different perspectives were apparent. For the most part, as long as we heard each other, we were okay leaving it like that. The roses smelled beautiful way more often than any pricks from the thorns, and our relationship was turning into a beautiful garden of roses.

Communication was to be key between Scott and me; learning to tell each other daily what we need and how we feel. We were learning that how we responded to each other's actions was often a reflection of how we felt about ourselves and our past stories that often confirmed this. It became much more apparent to me that I needed to be heard; keeping anything under the rug was not how I would be in this relationship. I made sure I was brave to speak about what I was thinking, no matter how dumb or minor it was. If it wasn't sitting well with me, I was going to say something.

Finding confidence to say what I was feeling and making sure that Scott was hearing it was a HUGE new awareness in my life that I needed to consistently take action on. I've struggled and struggled all my life with this, and now I've decided to make it a priority. No more holding back, even when I am scared. It is a *must*.

We had a conversation where Scott replied with a gruff and short remark, and it felt like he was somehow angry with me or disrespecting me in some manner. All I knew was that this didn't feel good. I was clear that the tone and the way he replied to me hurt me. When it was out on the table for both of us to see, Scott had apologized, and I reassured him that I needed to get it out of my system and it was about awareness and not blaming. Within minutes, we moved on and resumed our regular conversation. It is very important to me that we remain open and hear each other, even if it is hard to say and hear. We respect each other enough to do this.

Gentle on Myself

After our first dinner and hotel room on August 21—as I said, we booked flights back and forth from Calgary to Abbotsford—we took turns visiting each other's houses. I looked forward and yearned to have Scott in my arms each time.

When we would see each other at the airport, it was like our first date; always a long kiss and a strong embrace, and on a few occasions, dressing up (or should I say dressing with less sometimes). I enjoyed dressing up for Scott. He appreciated it, and I loved dressing sexy. I believe my strong attraction to Scott is because he shows me daily how much he loves and appreciates me. We always communicate how we feel. He always reminds me how beautiful I am; I remind him how sexy and gorgeous he is. I really love Scott. Through our actions and words, it is apparent.

During one of the flights on my way to Scott, I knew I was going to marry this man. With certainty, I wrote my vows to him. I had later revamped them in January and then again just before marrying him in July.

Vows - October 2021

Scott in the summer of 2021, I finally met you—the love of my life. I had a connection when I first saw you, when I heard you share your feelings, and I gravitated towards your joy for life and people. I soon realized I needed to be with you. Babe, you stole my heart, and you have graciously held it with unconditional love.

With you, Scott, I've found a love I have never experienced before. A love so honest and so genuine. A love I will never take for granted.

I knew very early that you, Scott, were exactly what my heart needed. We have balance. We have an emotional connection. We have a desire for each other. And we have a genuine love for each other to grow and to become better people. Scott, you are who I want to be with, grow old with, challenge and enjoy life with.

38

October 2021

I love you now and forever. You have forever changed my heart, and I thank you. I want to be your wife, your soulmate and your partner in life.

Forever yours, Lisa

Vows written within a month of meeting Scott

From flights, fights and writing vows, Scott also often challenged me. When I say I was challenged by Scott, he always saw more in me than I often saw in myself. I often saw the same in him, and I knew he was meant for bigger and better things too.

Scott challenged me to take scuba diving lessons. You see, he loved diving. He's been doing it for years and has been on about a hundred dives, usually down in Mexico. Well, this meant learning diving lessons online and then taking lessons in the local pool in Calgary. I was ready to take on a challenge. Actually, even if I wasn't ready, I was learning to take risks in my life, which was my way of moving forward and growing.

As a full-time teacher, I would work all day and then come home to put in the extra hours online to read all the scuba information and take the tests to pass the online part of the scuba diving certification. This I could manage, and I did. As for the in-pool classes, I was always stressed before each one and often found them difficult. I thought I was a great swimmer, and I am. However, the art of scuba diving requires a little more knowledge, patience and practice than I thought I could find within me.

I was doing these classes on my own (as Scott did not live with me yet in Calgary). I felt like a struggling student—a state difficult for me to swallow as a teacher. I struggled and struggled.

39

I struggled with the relaxed way of breathing through the regulator, getting the gear organized and knowing how to manage it, remembering all the little tips and skills that were to be remembered—like not inflating your Buoyancy Compensation Device (BCD) like a life vest as a way to get to the top. I was scolded for doing this once (or at least that is what it felt like). Again, I felt like I cowered, like the day the facilitator at the Ranch asked me, "How's that working for you?"

I was really getting in my head about how I was feeling about myself. I felt dumb and stupid about not being able to learn this skill of scuba diving with some confidence. It really shook me again and how little I believed in myself. I wanted to quit on several occasions and shared my feelings with Scott.

Scott always had so much faith in me, often way more than I (at that point) really had in myself. I really thought that I would not get this. I had to remind myself, and Scott often reminded me of this, too, "Be gentle on yourself."

This was one of the most important sayings Scott often said to me, and I would often send it back his way. He reminded me how we don't learn skills overnight. He reminded me that I was taking a big risk, a big challenge, and I was JFD'ing it (Just Fucking Doing It). I still use this phrase to this day—"Be gentle on yourself." Scott always knew what to say.

I continued my pool lessons and had to write the final exam paper. I didn't do so hot on that test; however, I passed. Sometimes I just need to be gentle on myself and remind myself that I am a great person. I struggle with things like anybody else, so be "gentle on myself."

I passed the knowledge and practice skills in the pool. I did it! Another example of taking some risks in my life and letting them be opportunities to grow. It's not just to say that I learned new skills and earned a passing score but what I really learned from this experience. I learned that I am only human. It takes time to learn new skills. When I struggle I dig really deep. When I struggle, I learn how strong, confident and brave I really am. I am proud of myself because I am fighting through fear. A big awareness in taking risks in my life.

CHAPTER 4

November 2021

What If?

Scott and I have been taking turns flying back and forth, making each other a priority. We were 100 percent committed to each other and strived to work on always remaining open and honest with each other. I truly desired the sense of security, safety and, most of all, love that I felt in his arms. His gentle nature and strong masculine hug were the perfect combination for my heart.

In one of my flights, though, a new thought came into my head (and my heart). All this travel meant more chances of an accident—a plane crash or something major that would hinder me from taking care of my 18-year-old daughter. I wanted her to know that she would be taken care of, and I knew that Scott did this for me and could be there for her. So, I opened a notebook in my carry-on. I wrote in haste.

I wanted to get it out on paper. I wanted the world to know. What if the plane went down now? I needed to sign my name to something, so it was known.

I quickly jotted down my thoughts. I wasn't sure when I would share such a request with Scott. I decided later that month to share the guardianship question with Scott. I'm still unsure why I didn't ask him when I initially wrote it on the plane. I'm not sure why I waited. Maybe we were so young in our relationship that such a request seemed too huge to put on someone's shoulder.

When I shared this request with Scott and asked him if he would take care (guardianship) of Brianna if something happened to me, I kind of just blurted it out and asked. He did not hesitate. He said, "Yes, I would look after Brianna without a doubt."

He reminded me that she may not accept it, as their relationship was so new, and she was only learning about him. This quick acceptance in looking after B was pure joy to my heart because I knew he was a good man—a good man to me and would be a good man to her. I pulled out my phone, got the guardianship thought off a piece of paper, and put it in the Notes app on my phone. I started to type, and I started to cry. Writing about my death sparked not only new feelings but also feelings that I had not been there enough for Brianna. Feelings that I did not say "I love you" enough. I still had so much to work on with her in terms of our relationship. I knew she deserved so much in life. This event was another lesson for me to ensure that my relationship with my daughter and son was a top priority.

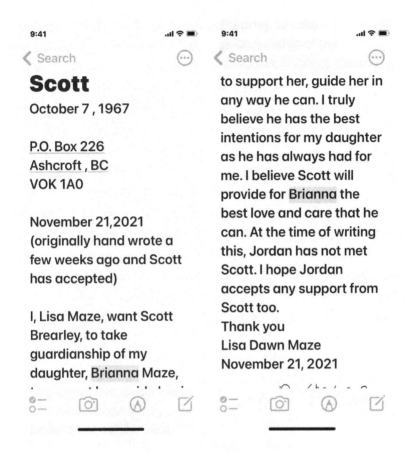

9:41 .ıl 📶 🔋

‹ Search (…)

Scott

October 7 , 1967

P.O. Box 226
Ashcroft , BC
VOK 1A0

November 21,2021
(originally hand wrote a
few weeks ago and Scott
has accepted)

I, Lisa Maze, want Scott
Brearley, to take
guardianship of my
daughter, Brianna Maze,

9:41 .ıl 📶 🔋

‹ Search (…)

to support her, guide her in
any way he can. I truly
believe he has the best
intentions for my daughter
as he has always had for
me. I believe Scott will
provide for Brianna the
best love and care that he
can. At the time of writing
this, Jordan has not met
Scott. I hope Jordan
accepts any support from
Scott too.
Thank you
Lisa Dawn Maze
November 21, 2021

Please take care of B

Growing Differences

At this point in my relationship with Scott, we were growing in strength
and learning new things about each other. He saw how I was often
riddled with self-doubt and lacked confidence in my abilities. I was
discovering new things about Scott too. You see, as we started to share
more about our pasts and where we came from, I started seeing a clear
picture of what Scott had to endure in his life. It supported some of
the actions and behaviours that I saw in him regularly.

One regular occurrence was the use of the F-word. The word *fuck* came out of his mouth as common as it is speaking the word *the* (the most spoken word in the English language). Okay, maybe not quite that much. Over these past two months, I learned more about his position on the word *fuck*. I've asked him at one point why he uses that word so much. He very confidently feels it's just a word. He's right; it is.

For me, with my Catholic upbringing and position as a teacher, I can probably count on all my fingers the times I've said the word (okay, probably a few more times than that. However, you know what I mean). For Scott, it seemed like it was part of every other sentence that came out of his mouth. I didn't see a lot of purpose for me to say it. The only reason might be a sense of frustration or excitement. However, to say it as a normal part of my conversation seemed a waste of a word, and yes, it was definitely not a word I heard very often.

I came to see how this was more normal for Scott because of his past and how it was common in what was all around him. I learned more about the chaos of his life, and I can only envision that the use of *fuck* was spoken in all those situations. From an unsettling family dynamic to drinking and drugs and hanging out with the gang on bikes. However, I presume that the word *fuck* was used by most of the people Scott associated with.

Scott learned early in his life that he needed to fight to survive. The word *fuck* was part of that survival story. A survival story that I am open to hearing and discussing with him. I assured him that over the time we had known each other I did not see his past. When I met him, I saw a man who covered all my requirements on the list (I wrote at the Ranch) of what I deserved in a partner.

I know that none of us are perfect. I know that I am not perfect. Like him, I desired to look more closely at myself and how I could learn new tools to move forward in my life. I still yearn for him to be heard, and I found that this F-word can get in the way. For me, and I'm sure many others, the F-word is not typically what you might hear in the white-collar space (the work sector I am familiar with). From my experience, the F-word meant you did not really find a better way to explain what you wanted to say or, in some way, you were in a state of emotional overload (be it excitement or anger). Either way, I didn't really associate with people who were typically using *fuck* in their everyday language.

I continue to be aware when he uses it, and I continue to be more aware that it's a normal part of his vocabulary. I really do not judge Scott at all for using the word in his everyday language. The only part that makes me sad is that others may not be as understanding and aware of this as I am and will immediately judge and dismiss him.

My own voice has been quiet most of my life, and I'm learning so much with Scott. I'm learning I have a voice. I'm learning I have needs that someone is respectful of. I'm learning. I'm learning.

Mom

November was the month I was fortunate to meet his "mother." I put that in quotation marks because I gained much insight into what really is a mother. A mother cares and would go to the ends of the earth for her baby.

Scott never really connected with his biological mother. He experienced hurt and mistrust from her. He decided, sometime during his life, that he needed to break ties with her. He no longer connected with her, and she never contacted him during the time I have been with him. When I said I met his mother, it's the lady who had been his mother since he was a late teenager in Alcoholics Anonymous. She met him at a meeting and took him under her wing. Because of her, he flourished in staying sober.

They have remained mother–son over the years, and I was so privileged to meet this lady over Zoom. You see, Scott had pretty much no contact with any of his family members, so I was excited to meet, Phyllis, the lady who stood by him. I think she was excited to meet me too. She was seeing Scott light up more. I think she knew he deserved the happiness she saw when we talked to her online. I was learning more and more about the people who really mattered in Scott's life—the woman he called his mother and those who he called his brothers, who again were not biological.

Scott has taught me that having these connections with people is a really deep thing for him. In his world it's not expected that blood is what makes your family. I was open to learning more, as I never had really thought about this before. My biological family was always a top priority to me. I had so much to learn about him. I learned to broaden my view of what makes a *family* a family.

Also during this month, Scott had to make a decision about his two Jack Russell dogs, Norton and Gemma, that he owned. Gemma was having a hard time and was aggressive towards other dogs when Scott was having friends look after them. So, Brianna and I decided to take both Norton and Gemma in to our house, as Scott was considering putting Gemma down due to her aggressive behaviour.

Brianna and I met Scott halfway, between his house in Ashcroft and mine in Calgary, and took his dogs back to Calgary with us. We thought that my calm-natured Alya would be good for Gemma and Norton, and my daughter was home to care for them all. The first few months with the three dogs were fun; however, Gemma continued to have aggressive tendencies. We later adopted her out to a caring family that had no other dogs, and she could get the attention she needed.

Gemma found her new home and Alya and Norton settled in together for the next several months together.

CHAPTER 5

December 2021

Early Christmas

Scott and I decided to take our first big vacation together at Christmas. We decided to travel to Cabo, Mexico. But before we headed off to Mexico, my kids and I enjoyed an early Christmas together.

This was my first Christmas in my new house as a *separated* woman from my former husband. In early December, when Scott had flown in for a weekend visit, Brianna, Scott and I took the time to get the decorations for the tree. Brianna and I agreed we liked having all the lights and decorations in a white hue (something we never had for twenty Christmases because my ex-husband really loved the look of multicoloured lights).

I invited my son, Jordan, and his girlfriend, Alannah, for a Christmas gathering. I love watching the two of them enjoy each other's company and the love that they share. I'm so grateful to celebrate Christmas traditions with them, like cooking dinner and opening presents. It was a great time, exchanging presents and playing Scrabble. Spending time with my kids is always a time I appreciate. I'm still learning how to always show my love to my kids. This has always been a very sensitive area for me, and I thrive on showing my love for them.

The next day, Scott arrived from Ashcroft, ready to go on our trip down south. I specifically arranged the day before to have my Christmas dinner and exchange presents before Scott came, as I wanted to let my kids know that I wanted to spend time with just them. I wanted to let them know that Scott didn't take their place and show them they could have my undivided attention.

I wanted Jordan to meet Scott before I went to Mexico. It is very important that my kids are comfortable with Scott. I believe they'd see what I see in him, and the big heart he has is what makes him a great man. So, when Scott arrived, I asked Jordan to meet him. It was a little awkward, but we thought it was a good first meeting. I was grateful that Jordan was open for the meeting. I know Scott appreciated that too.

Hello, Mexico!

On December 23, we headed to Mexico. I was excited for our getaway! This was our first big trip together. I wondered what he was like as a traveller. Did he stress over flying? Did he over-prepare? Under-prepare? Would we experience any new challenges? Would it be similar to what we have already experienced?

Well, we got on the plane, and we were both definitely excited during our four-hour flight—holding hands, cuddling close and just excited for our trip. We, unfortunately, had to wear masks while on the plane but made many opportunities to pull down the mask and sneak in several kisses.

Even though we had to wear masks on the plane to Mexico, we always found ways to show our affection. We made sure we showed each other how much we loved each other. I absolutely love showing Scott affection. I love kissing him. I love holding his hand. I love touching his body. I was excited for our getaway with a fun-in-the-sun place like Mexico.

For our trip, we rented a stick shift car. And since Scott had been to Cabo before, he found it comfortable making his way around and quickly remembered how to get around. With his truck-driving experience and motorcycling skills, he quickly got the lay of the land, and this gave me much comfort. I love how he steps into that with confidence.

We spent time enjoying each other, holding hands and getting our tan on! We toured beaches and restaurants, and hung out and went to a favourite coffee spot of Scott's—Cabo Coffee—for some yummy coffee. (We both love our coffees)

On the beach in Cabo San Lucas, Mexico

My Deep Dive

During our trip I decided to take my final scuba diving lessons and become an Open Water Certified scuba diver. I had taken those first lessons in the pool in Calgary, and now I was to get my final certification in Mexico.

Scott challenged me to become certified, and I say that with much gratitude and thanks. I appreciate that he has stepped up to become the little voice in my head that reminds me every day that *I am capable*. Because of his undying support for me and my abilities, I take more risks. No, I'm not immediately jumping out of airplanes when he challenges me; however, I am carefully examining why I may say no to challenges presented to me.

For example, I love moving to music and making up choreography to songs. I've always wanted to post my workouts online; however, I always had so much doubt about it. I now realize that when I have such doubt, I need to ask myself why. My immediate reaction to making such posts was, "What will I look like? Will I look stupid? Is it really good enough to share?" Well, that's all fear-driven—fear of not being accepted or liked, fear of not being good enough.

When I realized it's fear-based, I am able to find the confidence to "Just Do It" (as Nike branded). To make it more impactful, I use JFDI (yes, I've added the word *fuckin'*). So, I began to post some of my workout videos, and it felt great walking through my fear and taking that risk.

Now, I was very nervous and excited at the same time while learning the new skill of diving. I took my lessons in over two days. There were four dives in total, where I was shown a skill and then it was up to me to execute. Over all, I believe I did a good job. I was with another student, a teenager who spoke another language, so we didn't communicate much. The instructor spoke to him in his language and then spoke English to me. Talk about a patient instructor!

When I started the scuba lessons, I realized that this teacher (that's me!) was having a hard time being taught. In addition, my learned feelings of being underwater with a breathing apparatus in my mouth, knowing that was my only way of surviving, freaked me out. I had this fear for all the pool sessions. I needed to remember what Scott reminds me when I'm hard on myself: "Be gentle on myself." I needed to remind myself that anything new takes time. I eventually became more comfortable when I took the lessons in Mexico. It helped that the scuba instructor was patient and a great teacher.

Becoming a certified scuba diver in Mexico

On the fourth dive of my certification, I got to see a humongous school of fish swimming around us. It was incredibly cool, and I'm so glad I got to experience that. I got a little taste of how Scott described many of his scuba diving experiences. He often used the word *beautiful* to describe how he felt when he saw the underwater environment. I loved that about Scott. I loved how he appreciated the space and could so eloquently describe his experiences under the water. He's shared with me and others about a *sand fall* he's experienced. He describes it as a cool effect as if you are falling down into the unknown. Even Scott tells it way better than I do. I will highly credit him for telling a great story.

56

I was excited for Scott to have time to dive. You see, Scott already had about a hundred dives under his belt. He was experienced, and that shifted how I often felt about myself and my capabilities. When I talked to Scott about this feeling of being "behind him," he reassured me that it's not important and that my level of experience does not make him feel like he's holding back. He enjoys every dive, whether deep (because he can go deeper in the ocean with his level of certification) or not.

Scott and I further discussed how he looks forward to diving with sharks, and I'm excited for him to do that. However, at this point in my diving experience, it is so far from my interest. I honour his patience in my learning and his interest in doing more adventurous dives, like with the sharks or night diving.

Oh, I forgot to tell you! I have my Open Water Certification now!

CHAPTER 6

January 2022

Doing It Alone

Since it was Covid time, the protocol was to get a Covid test before boarding any plane back to Canada. We obliged and found a clinic where we could get our test done in the required time frame before leaving Mexico. Truth be told, I wasn't feeling great shortly after my scuba lessons, so the possibility of receiving a positive molecular test seemed inevitable! Sick or not, we did not want to spend time apart and continued to be intimate and sleep in the same bed.

We received an email from the clinic where we got our Covid test; I tested positive, and Scott was negative. We thought this meant he and I would be on an extended vacation in Mexico. Oh, I was wrong.

Out of respect for passing Covid on to someone else, we also had to cancel our New Year's Eve tickets to a dinner cruise with a five-course meal, music and what was to be our first New Year's together. I was extremely disappointed with these changes to our plans. Little did we realize what was really on the horizon for us. Little did I realize what the next four weeks would bring for me.

With the latest test results (and the craziness of all the Covid crap), we did our best to call the airline and enquire about changing our flights. Well, that was a nightmare. I think everyone on the planet was getting Covid, and the airlines were just inundated with flight changes. Since Scott tested negative, we drove the rental car to the airport on the day we were originally to return, January 4. We thought he could go in and rebook our flights for later, fourteen days after the initial test had passed.

We had all our luggage with us, as our plan would be to move to the next rental space where we would be quarantining together; a place with a little more room and space, so we could "enjoy" our time in quarantine in Mexico instead of being cooped up in a one-bedroom hotel room.

Scott made his way into the airport. Within minutes of enquiring about changing our flights, he returned to me and seemed somewhat hesitant with the update he had to give me.

The airline reps told him that since he tested negative, he would be able to return, and I would not be able to. WHAT? Could this be possible?

Ironically, just that morning, I made an agreement with him, not understanding that he would return to Calgary without me on that day. During breakfast, I bravely told him that whoever tested negative first would return to Calgary to look after the dogs and the house.

Well, that moment came that day, and Scott very quickly got his bags. He ran into the airport (since the flight was closing within minutes) after confirming I was okay with our decision, passing over the keys to the rental car, scrounging through pockets for any leftover American or Mexican money and assuring me that I was highly capable of doing this by myself in Mexico. Oh my gosh … was I really?

As it turns out, my additional days in Mexico were a true blessing; a lesson in growth that I give thanks for. I had to find my directions back to my newly rented hotel (with two rooms, two bathrooms, full kitchen/dining and living room), drive a stick shift car again, and figure out how to get my Wi-Fi to work so I could attend work meetings and get my report cards done. You see, the school board I worked for decided to wait an extra week to allow schools to make some decisions about Covid protocol, and teachers were asked to work online. This was beneficial to me, as I was stuck in Mexico. However, I needed to prepare for the several weeks that a substitute teacher covers for me while I was stuck in Mexico and later quarantined when I returned to Calgary.

I eventually made it home on January 15, not feeling well for a few days. I retested for Covid, upon the government's request, and tested positive again. I had to quarantine longer and never made it back into the classroom until January 21. What a big pain—all that organizing for a substitute teacher and following Covid rules when I felt great and ready to return earlier. However, the rules were not allowing me to return to work.

I realized during this whole ordeal that the combination of getting my physical body healthy a few years ago, doing the personal development work over the past few years, and Scott's undying support and love for me and my capabilities got me through it all. Having another human being letting me see how capable I am through their eyes is one of the most loving gestures I have received from Scott. He bragged to others about how he saw me grow and was proud. I love his public display of support and genuine love and care. This has been how he treated me since the first day we met. A true understanding that he believes I am capable—and I am capable. My feeling of confidence is beginning to grow every day still with hurdles along the way. Just like I truly believe he is capable and has such a strong and determined soul, I continue to always hear what he has to say with an open and caring heart.

The Shake-Up

I need to backtrack a little bit because I know you and I just got wrapped up in the Covid testing and Scott leaving me in Mexico by myself (Oh, you know I'm just pulling Scott's leg). You see, when Scott and I were in Mexico, the Personal Development group reached out to us to attend a course that was to begin at the end of January. We were informed that this course had an emphasis on achieving goals. We were to get support with goals we wanted to accomplish over a ninety-day period. We signed up for the ninety-day Pacesetters Leadership Dynamics (PLD) course. We were excited to do a course together, set goals and support each other in accomplishing them.

I knew Scott had goals he wanted to accomplish. During the PLD course, he was successful in earning his Life Coach certification from an online school. He set and achieved the goal of creating his website, Forward Walking Choices Coaching, and even got himself an email to match: Scott@ForwardWalkingChoices.com. I'm so proud of him for taking on such a big goal!

I had goals that I was excited about too. I wanted to earn my TEFL (Teaching English as a Foreign Language) as we planned to travel to

Thailand. Why Thailand, you ask? Well, we knew a few of Scott's friends there, and they talked about how they loved it. We thought, *What the heck… let's give it a go!*

Besides the TEFL academic goal, my physical goal was to achieve 390 seconds of three different body planks. I was also to do something new—I'd tithe my money and donate it to a worthy cause, my community center. Most importantly, I wanted to increase my connections with my two children by planning dates with them, as they are a priority in my life. I was excited to work on my goals and achieve success.

Little did we realize how much growth would happen during this PLD course. During that stay in Mexico, the lead coordinator encouraged us to join the course. We thought the purpose and course outline was setting and achieving goals, but the *real* focus that was promoted and practiced daily was not really made clear to the both of us.

As I said, we were both under the impression that it was a course to set goals and accomplish them through perseverance and support from the group. However, within hours of attending the first day of PLD on the last weekend of January, we were misled, and the focus of this course was skewed for us. The first assignment we were given was to call anyone (and everyone, it seemed like) in our contact list to sign them up to the three-day course (the one that Carolyn encouraged me to sign up for) and learn how to "convince" them to sign up. (Well, at least that's what it felt like for Scott and me.)

Oh my, you can say shit hit the fan for Scott, who is affected by those who tell him one thing but do another. This course stretched us in so many ways. He felt like he was misled, as did several other participants we later chatted with about the push on enrolment and not focusing on goal setting and accomplishments even though, I must mention, goals were talked about and celebrated.

With this bad taste in our mouths, we questioned each other—can we really handle this? Can we find it in each of us to support each other in this journey? Are we meant for each other? Are we enough for each other? Is this what we truly signed up for with each other? The PLD course, from the end of January to mid-May 2022, was one of the most turbulent times in our relationship yet, in more ways than one, the most rewarding.

As I look back now, PLD pushed me in a way I needed to be pushed. It got me uncomfortable, and I needed that. That's how I see it was beneficial for me. However, I know Scott still feels differently than I do about this course. He has said that PLD was quite damaging (at the time) to his mental health and on several occasions asked for support, however, it fell on deaf ears.

Straight from the get-go, there was a breakdown for Scott with the lead coordinator of this program. From the first weekend, Scott was negatively affected by her. He really wanted to be flexible and make this goal setting work. He had told the coordinator early on in our discussions about the fact that he often worked until 7 p.m. for his job. If he needed to join any online events, he may be late or may have to join while working. He approached the coordinator and felt that she abruptly gave him the cold shoulder, showing no sense of flexibility from her end. This really rubbed him the wrong way as he attempted to approach her with a solution-based mindset.

After some time in the course, some information led Scott to understand her a little more. However, for him, it never really excused her stance of "I'm better and know more than you. In the end, I will get you to do whatever I need you to do." Well, maybe it's not her exact words, but it's that sentiment that Scott heard from her mouth the first weekend when he said she literally put her out in front of his face to disregard his solution. It left Scott with a really bad taste in his mouth about feeling supported on his journey of growth.

Scott put a lot of energy into the mistrust he felt from her, which shook our own relationship. I saw how he let her rob his energy and how he had difficulty moving past that. I saw how his childhood experiences shed light on this current challenge. I started to see more that he had so many people he could not trust in his life. I began to see that those people, like his family who were supposed to nurture and take care of him, had created an environment of mistrust and uncertainty for him. I could see, on many occasions, that what he thought about others was all coming up for him again. Events were happening that reinforced his lack of trust in others.

Scott builds relationships on trust. He describes the lead coordinator as someone who just pulled the rug out from under him, leaving him with what he had thought and known all his life: Don't trust those in charge.

His doubt in the lead coordinator gave Scott a tainted feeling about the course. Any notion that this course had a group of fellow supporters fell short for Scott. This helped me see that Scott still had many layers to peel back and discover. I knew it would come for him, and I strived to be patient in supporting my beautiful man in his journey. We were at another point in our relationship, and that was a new awareness for me. I saw how Scott struggled with mistrust and dishonesty, which was a tough hurdle for him. I saw how this hits him at the core of his being.

This gave me more insight into how much he had these experiences as a child and how this affected him as an adult. I started to see more layers of how he was altered in his early life and how his only way to get through life was to "fight back." He needed to survive the chaos and uncertainty he saw all around him. However, because of those childhood experiences, Scott is honest, open and says it like it is. There is no fluff with him, and I see that every day. I love Scott and his open-book way of living.

How would we manage these next ninety days? Will we figure it out? How will we figure it out? Will there be doubt? Will Scott have a breakthrough? Will I? Will confidence shine for me, finally?

CHAPTER 7

February 2022

My First Costume

In February, Scott and I ventured into a new territory. Scott was no longer working, suffering from trauma and mistrust from work, and he was now living in Calgary (the big, boring city—from Scott's point of view and mostly in terms of riding a motorcycle because there are no great roads to ride on) with me and Brianna. This new living arrangement, Scott not working, and the stress of PLD stretched us thin some days.

With the expectations of PLD, Scott found himself in bouts of depression, and I was wondering how to support him in those challenges. I also found myself having so many of my own buttons pushed during this ninety-day course. We were told on many occasions that our buttons are meant to be pushed, so we can grow and learn from them. All these new challenges for Scott and me pushed the envelope on what our relationship could handle and how we would deal with it all.

With the crazy time schedule of PLD, we found ourselves being a little more deliberate about date nights, or at least just making time for each other. We found this a little challenging, as we had all the time in the world to spend together and enjoy each other up to now. This was a new stressor for us.

During this course, we were inundated with WhatsApp and Messenger notifications. I ignored them all day, as my priority was to focus on my teacher job five days a week, from 8 a.m. to 4 p.m., and not be on my phone checking for updates. But when the teaching day was over, I checked on enrolment updates, encouraged my "teammates" in the group and supported however I could. For Scott, the constant dinging of notifications started to drive him a little crazy. For a guy getting frustrated and feeling the stress of PLD, he eventually opted to pull himself off the apps. If people wanted to connect with him, they needed to call him. As I said earlier, Scott often had difficulty with technology, and texting was not the best way to communicate with him.

With daily phone calls to coaches and check-ins with a group buddy, we struggled to find great quality time together. We were either attending a meeting online, preparing for a presentation or achieving some new goal. We had less time for intimacy in bed in the mornings, too, because we needed to make these coach and buddy calls before I had to head to work. While I was at work, Scott was home, even more stressed over working on this online coaching course. Doing an online course both drained him mentally and stretched him to his limit on many days.

The months between January and May were all a blur yet still so clear with many learnings. As mentioned, PLD was meant to push buttons, and when in the land of discomfort I had many moments of growth.

I knew one of my goals early on was to feel more confident. I donned my *confidence costume* whenever I needed to call on it. For many months it remained as a costume, and confidence was not innate in me.

The costume analogy came from an activity we did during a PLD weekend, where we were asked to dress up as someone we admired. Then, we were to speak as that person and talk about how great they are doing! The subject was not important. However, the activity was. In front of the group, we were to walk in like the person we admired and then stand on a stage and act just like them. Well, the person I chose was Angelina Jolie. Why? Not too sure. However, I have always thought of her as a confident, well-poised person.

So, there I was, strutting down the aisle as Angelina Jolie. The aisle was filled with the PLD participants down each side. I was sexy and confident and spoke throughout the required amount of time. Wow! I did that! I looked confident! I spoke off the cuff! I didn't waiver! I JFDI!

That day, I was reminded by my coach, Alex, that for now I need to pull out that confidence costume from the closet so I can make confidence a normal part of my life.

He was right! You see, the coaches of this course were all volunteers. I appreciate the time that Alex gave me and what he saw in me.

Alex Lam, you were monumental in my growth over those ninety days. Thank you.

One of the requirements of this course was to host an online presentation about the three-day weekend course offered on personal development. Scott and I decided to host a presentation together. He and I quickly put in our request to present first and get it over with.

Well, that quick action put us into another frenzy of craziness. We had to contact as many people as possible to get them to attend. In all our spare time (NOT!), we called, texted, emailed and chatted with friends, family and acquaintances to attend our online evening presentation. It wasn't as easy as just posting it on Facebook. We needed to call and talk to people, provide them with a link to the online event or, even better, sign them up right there and then as we spoke to them. It was all a bit much. However, I did it, and I believe we got about twenty-ish guests to join us online.

On February 11, I was scheduled for a minor surgery and thought this was a good time to don my confidence costume and speak to a stranger in the waiting room at the hospital. I am still surprised that I found a sense of brevity (my confidence costume) to speak to a complete stranger about my story and how this three-day course started it all. I felt like I did a great job that day, sharing my journey with this other woman who was also waiting to be called in for her surgery, how this personal development has changed my life, and how I have found this amazing man.

The lady I spoke with was intrigued by my story, and I was able to send her (via text) the link to the presentation. Even though she did not attend, I truly appreciate that experience and understand that I am capable. Wearing this confidence costume is great practice for me and for moving forward.

I knew that if I wore this costume enough, it would begin to be Lisa and not just a costume I put on. So, while we were hosting our online presentation on February 25, I donned my confidence costume again. Scott and I were asked to present our own personal stories of growth. I didn't truly believe yet that I could speak with any eloquence or hold a consistent thought, so I made some brief notes on my phone and positioned it so the online audience would not see it, and that was how I shared my growth story.

After the presentation, I was thanked for my heartfelt speech. No one commented that they felt I was reading from some cheat notes. I knew it was baby steps for me at this point, and that was okay.

Scott also spoke during the online presentation. However, he told me he wasn't really in it. Even though, at that point, he was struggling with his journey inside, Scott was still able to hold the audience's attention and give a compelling speech. With no notes and with such ease, he told how this personal development work propelled him forward through his many struggles in life.

During this ninety-day course, we were expected to speak in front of our PLD group (about thirty participants) on many occasions and think on the spot. I realized that I used this confidence costume a lot and was definitely feeling more confident. I knew I still needed much more practice. To this day, I still need to pull that costume out of some back closet, and that's okay.

CHAPTER 8

March 2022

The Struggle of Letting Go

During these four months, others often commented on how Scott and I were doing as a couple on this journey. Yes, as a couple it was both challenging and extremely rewarding. My PLD goal was to find my own strength and confidence—something I longed for all my life.

How would I step up in my life, speaking for my needs and his? What would that look like? How do I respect myself and him at the same time? How do I operate within this group? It was all a little confusing and, still to this day, not really clear. However, I learned that he needed to figure his own shit out, and I needed to do the same. All at the same time, he knew I continued to love him for him and the journey he was on.

I knew that open communication and honesty were the *only* way to go. I knew that talking about our challenges was key, even if I didn't know what to do. Scott often was insightful in his questions and supported our growth together. He is a very persistent soul who has learned to survive in this world a certain way, and I was learning how he did this. All through this time, I loved him every minute of the day, even with the struggles of not seeing eye to eye or having different opinions such as the benefits we were getting from this ninety-day course.

During PLD, Scott flew to New Mexico to attend a Men's Leadership course. He later told me he learned a lot about himself. He enjoyed the course and got great benefits from it.

In regards to the men's course, Scott sometimes wishes he had attended the Men's Leadership course with a clearer head on his shoulders instead of using it as a way to get away from the PLD stress.

While Scott was down in New Mexico, I was in the process of filing for my divorce after a year of separation. I was struggling about feeling confident and properly completing all the divorce paperwork, meeting my former husband at the courts to submit the paperwork and in a place of feeling small. I really struggled not having my number-one supporter by my side.

It was my spring break, and I was off work for a week. I thought I was going to master my to-do list and get the divorce stuff done, and the divorce process would be well on its way. Instead, the paperwork was incomplete, and it dragged on into the latter part of that week off.

I put myself in a hole of despair and considered quitting PLD due to the stress of feeling like a failure when dealing with my former husband

and figuring out the divorce paperwork. I struggled not having Scott there to support me in navigating my negative feelings—feelings of despair and emotional turmoil that seemed to be taking over me. I emailed Scott more than usual to get these emotions out of my body and reached out to a few of our PLD members. However, it was a struggle that I needed to contend with and learn from.

Since I was challenged with applying for my divorce that week, I decided to reach out to my therapist, Kimberly, whom Scott introduced me to. Early in our relationship, about a month or two in, Scott and I were talking (one night in bed) either about my previous relationship or my challenges in fully connecting with my children. Scott mentioned I should consider talking with Kimberly, and he was right.

Kimberly is a trauma therapist. Scott had met with her for about a year before meeting me. He spoke highly of her and the great work that she has done with him over Zoom. Scott often comments that she takes over where other therapists leave off. For Scott, understanding his trauma from when he was young was a key to moving forward. For me, my trauma stemmed from my past stories that I allowed to be reinforced throughout my life—that I am not worthy, not enough, not smart and not capable of properly sharing my thoughts and feelings.

Kimberly helped me visualize how I would manage to deal with being around my former husband. So, with an emphasis on my physical health, personal development and Scott's love, I have added Kimberly to my arsenal of success!

During that break from school, I took on one more big emotional roller coaster. I knew I needed to look through and downsize the many boxes of my children's precious mementoes, like the pictures they drew in school when they were little or the homemade gifts they made for me. I knew I kept too much. Although, at the time, I never thought I could keep too much of the precious things they gave to me.

I relived so many memories—my son Jordan's visual journal entry of sleeping over at his friend's house for the first time or the scribble on a purple piece of paper from my daughter. It was time to decide what to keep and what to let go, which was difficult. If I questioned or hesitated about it, I knew it was time to let go. I closed my eyes, kissed the item and either recycled it or tossed it in the garbage. I needed to acknowledge that I was sad to let it go and then just say goodbye.

This was a tiring and emotionally draining procedure for me. Scott was not around, and it allowed me to grieve my past relationship in some way. I needed to do this for myself. I needed to start letting go of some of my baggage from my first marriage, and this process allowed me to move forward.

I kept a few items for my kids and made sure to pass them on when I saw them next. They appreciated some of the sentiments and that I did not just pass it all over to them.

When Scott returned from New Mexico, I saw a renewed man. I missed him dearly during this time (of no internet connection) and continued to email him daily about my love for him and the challenges I was going through. I knew he would not get those emails until he had left the course after the week; however, emailing him daily was therapeutic for me.

The Big Blow-Up

After Mexico and March Break, we were at the next PLD event. We slept over at a retreat location where we had activities wherein, again, buttons were pushed and we were stretched to our emotional capacity. The purpose of those activities was always to ride the crazy emotional waves and have better clarity by the end.

For the most part, this happened. However, sometimes the waves were so turbulent that the feeling of drowning was very close. On one weekend, Scott, who was very successful at enrolling others into the initial three-day course, had signed up a certain number of participants, which meant a level of recognition from the establishment. Well, he did not receive it. They denied him the acknowledgement because they were unsure of the numbers. Naturally, Scott found this unacceptable and felt (again in his life) let down, as he has been let down far too often.

It was a big blow out; Scott stormed out of the building, blurting out several curse words, and his huge frustration was apparent. Again, how would I support him? I knew, in some manner, my voice and my strength in me were all being tested. I was learning what it meant to really be a partner. I was growing in this way, that is for sure.

We had had an earlier challenge in PLD before this happened. Scott was outwardly frustrated, and we talked about it after the dust had settled. He said he just wanted to be left alone in moments like that to collect his thoughts. As I said before, communication was key for us, and discussing what the other needs was very important. So when he "exploded" during the PLD weekend where he was not acknowledged for the enrolments he made, I let him walk away. However, the worry and fear that he might totally leave the course was real for me.

I knew this man deserved love and acceptance from the group—
something I knew he longed for. I reminded those close to me that
he needed space, so he could decompress. Scott had come very far
with realizing many things about himself and how he reacted in that
situation. His reactive nature has changed a lot over the last several
years. He has been learning to be aware of stressful moments; walking
away to take time without anyone looking over his shoulder was what
he needed.

That weekend, Scott really wanted to quit. On location, the ladies
and men slept in separate residences. Scott had made sure his bed
was in his own area, and I chose to sleep with Scott (fully dressed, in
respect to those around) in the men's residence that night, with no
one making any fuss over this situation. He needed reassurance that
he was loved and that I heard and saw him for the person he was. I
could see that he was really hurting.

In the end, I knew both the men and women in PLD knew I
supported Scott the best way I could, and he and I were a strong
couple who would work together with much love and respect for each
other's journey.

Learning about each other and how we would support each other in
coping with stressful situations was a big learning curve for us during
the ninety-day course. Throughout my life, I knew I lived a rather low-
key (boring) lifestyle, and that was okay. However, I've always felt I
was a spontaneous person who never really took an adventure in her
life. I met Scott for a reason. I've started this personal development
work for a reason.

But, Can't, Try

My PLD mantra was, "I am a sensual, intelligent, eloquent leader, spontaneously taking risks in my magnificent life *now*." I appreciate this understanding and reminder that I am a highly capable person and deserve all the love life offers. This mantra was created from those insecurities I believed about myself. The part about the eloquent leader was about how I've always found it difficult to speak and share my thoughts and ideas in a flowing or interesting way.

In the course, we were challenged to think before we spoke and be clear about what we were saying. The challenge that was presented was to delete three words from our vocabulary, as they often undermined our belief in the message we were communicating. Those three words are: *but, can't* and *try*. Well, this was surely a challenging goal for me. Not only did I struggle to share my thoughts, now I needed to stop and think about not using these words.

It was an eye-opener, and I still strive not to say them (and that's why you will find very few of those words in this book too!). I have trained my brain to say what I need with clarity and a positive mindset. What comes out of my mouth is important, and I am learning to stop and think more about what I want to say. I once believed that my opinion and thoughts had not mattered, and this challenge has pushed me to step up in my thinking and sharing what I thought.

If you are reading this book—and I know you are—take on this challenge, even just for an hour. Do not say these three words: *but, can't, try*.

When you say the word *but*, you negate your first thought and make an excuse. For example, "I want to take piano lessons, but my fingers are too short." Instead, you could say, "I will take piano lessons and see how I do."

For the word *can't*, it's just a negative mindset. If you say, "I can't do maths very well," the positive mindset would say, "I struggle with algebra, so I'm going to Google a video to explain it to me." It's all about being solution-oriented!

For the word *try*, it's a cop-out. We often say, "I will try to use my left hand because my right hand is sore." Well, change the mindset. When you use that T-word, it says to your body that you are not sure or don't have a clear goal that you will accomplish. A positive mindset might say "I will use my left hand to open the jar, and if it does not work I will ask my daughter to open it."

I know it may sound like a bunch of nonsense to you. What does a couple of words have to do with you and how you feel about yourself? One way I like to think of it is this: Which is better for you?

1. I am dumb, and my ideas are stupid. Or,
2. I am excited to learn new things, and I have cool ideas!

I hope you said the latter is healthier for you. However, I know it's not always easy. I had thought the first option about myself most of my life and still continue to consciously make the latter a priority.

One of our goals during PLD was going to Thailand. Well, for me, this meant a big and scary decision that I had to make. I had to approach my principal with the fact that I needed his approval to take the year off from my teaching position. I had to apply for a Leave of Absence from my twenty years with the Calgary Teaching Board and felt like I was throwing my planned future right out the window. I would (like so many) work until I retire, and that's it. That's all.

I was pushed out of my comfort zone, out of my norm, out of boring and into living—and that was freakin' scary. I knew that with Scott I could handle anything—I realized this early in our relationship. I would say that within the first month (or even earlier), my gut instinct was very clear to me—with Scott by my side, anything could be solvable and figured out. I'm not sure why I felt this so clearly with Scott. Maybe it was because of how certain he was that I could achieve anything I wanted. However, I still had my own fears and worries about making big life changes and decisions. What would my family think? How would I have enough money? Ah, there goes the "plan."

I've come to realize that I didn't have a plan to continue to teach straight through to my retirement. No, I had a plan to take a break and re-evaluate my life. This understanding only came to me several months after applying for the leave.

Stepping Out of My Comfort Zone

During this ninety-day course, I had to pull out my confidence costume more than once. We were asked to step out of our comfort zone and talk to complete strangers (or friends and family) to introduce them to the idea of attending the three-day weekend course that started all the personal development for Scott and me. This was a strenuous requirement for me.

I chose to pursue people while I was out. For example, I pre-ordered groceries to pick up at the local Safeway. Once I got there, I was told that Amber would be out shortly with my groceries. I mustered up a conversation about my recent engagement to this amazing man and how this was possible because of the personal development work I've done on myself and Scott on himself. Would she be interested in me sending her info on taking the course? Could I *convince* her to trust me and take the course?

This was somewhat of an awkward conversation. However, I knew I needed to be stretched in what I thought I was capable of doing. I also needed to still be okay with sharing such an idea and possibly being rejected on promoting this course.

You see, I learned that not everyone is ready to hear what I have to offer. Not everyone is in a space where they can accept my idea. Not everyone—and, really, most people—are open to having another human being talk about growth and spending money on themselves and just going for it!

I had many of these conversations over the ninety-day period because I cared about other people and wanted them to have the same opportunity and chance for growth like I did. I talked to a lot of friends and family about such an opportunity because I cared for them immensely and wanted more for them. This didn't always come through that way, however. I learned that I often spoke about the course like a sales pitch, and I still was learning how to express myself with heart. This was something I was beginning to learn. I was beginning to be confident and not have to wear a costume quite as much.

I often lacked emotional connection and an outward display of feelings. Throughout my life, I learned to hide many of my feelings and did not feel at ease in expressing myself. When I did, I wasn't taken seriously or felt supported or acknowledged or respected for what I was expressing. So, being with Scott has been a real eye-opener for me. He hears me, listens to me and really wants me to be heard. He supports me in being clear and confident in my words. He questions me when I sound doubtful or include doubting words. He asks me to sometimes rethink what I am saying and throw away the self-doubt comments that often drip out of me like water from a leaky hose.

I've learned a really important understanding that I truly cherish with Scott. He has supported the fact that expressing myself is a really great thing. I've never cried and broken down so much in my life than I have over this year of love. Scott supports me in the emotional journey I've been on, and I am truly grateful for this sign of love and acceptance from him. Scott supports me and allows a space for me to do this. I now realize that I truly appreciate that in my partner. Scott is definitely my partner.

During this ninety-day course, I said we were stretched to new limits of overcoming fears and blasting through them. We were sent out on a mission. I was to ask any stranger if they would like to join me for lunch, and I would pay for them. REALLY? Could I do this?

I started on this mission with a positive outlook. I think I may have had that confidence costume just barely swung over my shoulder. With this mission in mind and my confidence level on high, I brainstormed where to find this person that I would have lunch with: Which store would I find some of the most caring people? As I looked around the shopping mall area, I saw it—the pet store!

I ventured in and looked around at the shoppers. I thought, at first, that I would be looking for just one person to ask out and not a family (as we were given a budget). So, I found Jenn, a kind young lady shopping for her two dogs and buying supplies for her fish at home. I sparked up a conversation and went straight to the point.

I said, "I'm out today doing brave things in my life, and this is one of them. Speaking to a complete stranger and hoping I could take you out for lunch. I'm actually recently divorced and stepping into some fears of taking small risks like this. I know it might sound weird, but are you hungry and can I buy you some lunch?"

Crazy! Did that really come out of my mouth? Was I brave to do this? Yes, I was. Well, with that, we were on our way in our own cars and over to a '50s diner close by. I shared about my life with Jenn and how I had been separated from my husband. I was excited to share about the loving relationship I'm in with Scott and the whole spiel on how we met through personal development.

It was so great getting to meet Jenn. We had planned to walk the dogs at a later date. She was so gracious that when we met again, she brought me a lovely birthday card and a Starbucks gift card. I learned that taking these small risks enriched my life and supported me in broadening who I was and what I was capable of doing.

CHAPTER 9

April 2022

The Crown

It is getting close to May, and PLD is wrapping up. It's time to celebrate all the accomplishments and goals we worked so hard to achieve. It was a course with so many challenges, so much button-pushing. We worked our emotional capabilities to the nth degree and survived. We witnessed ourselves and others struggle, have a new awareness of ourselves and establish new understandings. All this hard work deserved a party! Finally, right? Well, this, too, presented a new challenge for Scott and me. Something we needed to work through—the party was taking on a different meaning for both of us.

Throughout this course, we prepared for and even raised money for this end gala event, where we would celebrate ourselves and our group members for their courageous efforts, working through many challenges and surviving. This was an event I was looking forward to. I had worked extremely hard on multi-multi-multi-tasking and realized I may not have been cut out for the go-go-go of PLD. I was looking forward to my recognition for working so hard. I was actually not overly concerned about public acknowledgement through awards; I was just ready to breathe again.

I appreciated the personal level of congrats from other members at meetings, texts and emails. However, I never really strived for the most enrolments or to be the most influential in the group. I did not feel worthy of such acclamations and did not like being made the centre of attention. However, I was truly grateful for my amazing efforts during this ninety-day course. I deserved to give myself a pat on the back via this gala.

This gala event was special to me. It was a chance to dress up and show up as a more confident woman. A woman who was new to me. A woman I was showing up as for the first time. A beautiful woman showing up differently. I was excited for her!

I found my dress at Value Village, a second-hand store. The dress was cherry red, a colour that was bold—something I typically was not. However, this dress wasn't all ready for me to wear when I found it. I had to see its potential. My daughter and I were out shopping at Value Village (if you say it in a fancy way, it sounds like an expensive store—*Valooo Village*. A great friend, Corynn, told me this a few years ago), and I pulled the dress (or what I thought was a dress) off the rack and showed it to Brianna.

We both thought, *Wow!* However, we were a little perplexed by the extremely long slit that seemed to travel each side all the way up to the waistline. I knew it needed work. It was perfect, and it would be the dress.

April 2022

"Well, at least let's buy it and try it on at home," Brianna suggested, as Covid didn't allow us to try it in-store. It didn't break the bank at CDN$38.00, and I could return it for a refund if it didn't fit.

My daughter tried it on first when we arrived home and twirled around, making sure to rearrange the long lace train as she repositioned each time. I knew right there and then it was the dress. I tried it on after her and said yes to the dress (as the popular saying goes). The next day, I took it to the seamstress, and they perfected it with a new slip on the inside to match the cherry red. It was so elegant and exuded sexiness and confidence. I found the perfect cherry red, suede, high-heeled Guess shoes to match.

With my excitement for the gala and celebrating my success, I was stoked to be accompanying my incredible man. He had previously purchased a tuxedo for his Men's Leadership course. What a handsome man Scott is in his tuxedo, and if I do say so myself, we make a stunning couple. I was proud of Scott, as he bought his first suit and tuxedo over the past several months—moving on up, eh?

I was excited and thrilled to be by this incredible man as he stood beside me through our many accomplishments and challenges. Even though this evening was set up for a night of celebrations and acknowledgements, there was a looming event that was to happen with Scott that had been in the works for almost a month now. You may remember how Scott had a falling out with the lead organizer the first weekend of PLD.

Over the course of PLD, he had discovered that she was referred to as the Queen on a document roster that we all had our names on. Scott took it upon himself to meet her persona and be called King. He thought that purchasing a crown to signify his "king-ness" would be a great way to show her that he does not back down and does what he wants.

87

Scott's plan to wear the crown during our gala evening made for probably one of our first unsettling disagreements. This disagreement happened a few weeks before the gala. When Scott was away in Ashcroft, we video-called, and I was feeling a sense of unease regarding this crown.

I was uncomfortable with the feeling that this was like an eye for an eye sort of scenario—the idea of wearing a crown with his tux would really show the "Queen" that Scott doesn't back down. I felt conflicted about watching him go through his own discoveries of what he was (or wasn't) capable of letting go and my concerns over my boyfriend choosing to wear the crown without hearing my concerns or feelings about it. I discovered early on in my relationship with Scott that sweeping my thoughts under the rug was not going to be any sort of norm in any relationship I'd be in anymore. So, I chose to talk to him about my thoughts.

While talking to Scott over our video call, I had to reassure myself over and over again (oh, self-talk is so important) that I need to always share what I'm feeling, and not having a solution to it was okay. I've learned to listen to my gut (and my heart). If something was not sitting right on the inside, I needed to share it with Scott. If this was going to be a problem, then our relationship was either not going to work or we had a lot of work ahead of us to make this relationship a success.

Well, Scott had purchased the crown at this point, and bringing up my concern made him quite frustrated that I did not bring it up sooner. I didn't have a real answer to that question. However, I knew at that moment I was feeling what I was feeling, and I was going to share it.

I wanted to know how he envisioned that evening happening. When would he wear the crown—all night or just on his entrance?

Would it be embarrassing to him? To me? How would I handle the questions about it? Would I be seen as defending him? Would it appear that I was in agreement with his actions (as I knew that this was something I would not do)?

When I asked, I felt a lot of angst from him, like he saw me putting him into a corner and that I should have stated my thoughts earlier (before he spent money on the crown). I was confused for some time. However, I still knew I needed to share my concerns, and no, I did not have a solution for that evening. I was not there to tell him what to do; I just needed to be heard.

As I shared more over our video chat, I could tell he was growing distant from our conversation. We left it alone at the moment. We said goodnight and signed off, knowing we would need talk about it later. That moment terrified me. I was sharing and he was pulling away, as if he was doubting our relationship. He could not be clear about how he saw the evening going, and this made me nervous. I was equating the fact that I had shared my feelings and concerns with him and felt like we were now at odds because of it.

After we ended the call and said we would talk in the morning, I knew I had to decide how I was going to show up that evening, whatever he decided to do about wearing this. I have learned over our PLD time that I needed to remain open to having a fun evening because I choose to have a fun evening. I knew I had to remain open.

That's all there was. I had to remain open; open for fun, open for celebrating. Open.

Small Stretches

PLD time seemed like it was such a crazy, busy ninety days. However, I have so much I appreciate from the whole experience. I learned how influential Scott really is. When his heart is in it, he can move mountains. I saw him encourage and support friends in taking the three-day weekend course and loved them so much in the process. It was incredible to see the depth of his caring with those friends. I admired his ability to confidently share with others and encourage them to better themselves. His level of certainty is very inspiring.

For myself, I was able to encourage my friend, Magdalena, to sign up for the three-day course. I was excited for her and looked forward to seeing how the course may benefit her. I had worked with Magdalena at Earl Grey Elementary School for many years. I was so proud of her for stepping into this challenge.

During Magdalena's time in the three-day course, we had the opportunity to congratulate her on taking this personal development for herself. I asked Scott to accompany me in celebrating Magdalena, and he said he wouldn't miss seeing that she is loved and cared for by us. When she saw us standing there to congratulate her, she got emotional. We were both crying with her with so much joy and love. I was filled with happiness for her and, at the same time, was so proud to have this caring man beside me to congratulate her. It meant a lot for me to be there for Magdalena, and I'm proud to have my boyfriend support someone who I knew deserved our love and acknowledgement.

While stretching my capabilities and bravery in myself, I also found myself doing things without recognition, like talking to strangers to see if they would like to expand their lives and take the three-day weekend course of personal development and being okay when they said, "No, thank you," and not taking it personally. I really did step out of my comfort zone. Quiet, little ol' me who had no opinion usually thought, *Don't rock the boat.* I knew I was changing. I knew I was changing for the better.

During the ultimate time of stretching myself, one big struggle for me was stepping up to lead our PLD group's online weekly meeting. Everyone was to take their turn to run a meeting and follow the expected meeting guideline.

You see, Covid put a wrench in how the PLD classes were being conducted. Our group was one of the first hybrid groups taking two big cities, Vancouver and Calgary, and combining them. Since people could not gather in person at the first of Covid, they shifted to online classes. Then as the restrictions started to loosen, a combination of part-in-person and part-online was held. With this slow momentum of getting back to some sense of "normal," numbers were not viable to hold in just one city. When our two cities were combined, the Vancouverites were asked to travel (almost once a month) to Calgary to attend events. This was demanding for many.

The number of online events, presentations and meetings also put another stress on our group. The fact that people were not really meeting up (in person) to support each other was also another stressor. Personally, another stress was that Scott felt the wrath that others did not understand him, did not connect with him and did not have the time to give support. Scott was so frustrated with how incohesive our group was and that he was not gaining anything from it.

Still, Scott and I both agree that we did gain some wonderful friendships from this group. One of the kind souls we met was our dear friend, Audrey. We met Audrey during the week-long course where Scott and I met and continued to stay connected with her. Audrey is a kind, warm soul who sees Scott for the loving man he is. She often called and talked to him (as per his request—call him). Audrey has supported me in supporting Scott and has seen how our love is so healthy, genuine and amazing.

Anyway, each member had to facilitate a meeting, and it was my turn. This was a real challenge for me. Not only had I convinced myself that I struggled to speak in front of adults, I knew our group was struggling, and I knew that Scott was struggling too.

I looked to keep the meeting positive, yet you could feel the tension building during the meeting. I could slowly feel myself drowning, and it felt like I was letting this meeting sink. I was fortunate to have a buddy during these ninety days—Shirley. Oh, Shirley. I was grateful for her and my coach Alex.

When this program began at the end of January, we were all together in a room and asked to stand up in front of thirty other people and find someone who scared us. I hesitantly looked around and spotted this gorgeous, well-dressed and poised blond lady who personified confidence and charisma. There is the person who scares me. I walked to her and said something to the effect of, "I choose you."

She kindly obliged. We were told whoever we picked would be our buddy for the remainder of the course. I knew I was in for some challenges and scary things. I knew that I had chosen the right person.

During the meeting, my buddy Shirley backed me up to keep the meeting going and acknowledged that there was stress and tension; however, this meeting was not for venting and should remain on the timeline set out. Sticking to a timeline was always done with integrity and respect for everyone's time. With that comment from Shirley, the meeting went on. Scott bowed out of the meeting in some disgust, as I believe he felt that he was not being heard and ultimately being dismissed once again in his life. I believe a few others had similar feelings and signed off the online meeting.

I struggled a lot after this meeting. I felt like a failure, as I hoped to keep it positive and boost morale in the group. Instead, I felt I let the group down and let Scott down too. I really struggled with remaining positive and still respect Scott and his frustration with the group. We continued to talk and share about our daily stressors, and I always kept space available for Scott to feel heard.

I did have several group members text me about how they appreciated me facilitating the meeting and how I persevered to keep it positive and on time. At the time, I felt like I did my best running that meeting. I was brave to take it on and had the group's best interest at heart, which I believe most of the group saw. In retrospect, I can confidently say that anyone who had trouble with the meeting was their perspective and had nothing to do with me.

So, taking risks like leading the group meeting was big for me. Learning that I had the group's best interest at heart was all I needed. I knew I was not to look at this one experience as a reason to think I was going to be a weak speaker forever.

I was learning that taking these risks was all for growth. I was becoming a more confident person, more resilient and more aware of what was important to me. The relationships in my life were becoming a prominent thought. I was learning how to let the important people in my life know how much I love them and wanted them in my life. My best friend, Sandra, was one of those people.

My Best Friend, Sandra

I grew up in the small province of Prince Edward Island, Canada. My little community consisted of five houses, and across the road and up the hill was my friend Sandra. I have always considered Sandra my BFF (best friend forever). We were tight in our younger years. Then, boyfriends, marriages and me moving across the country happened. However, we never really let go of the fact that we had made this special connection many years ago.

You see, as an Islander, leaving such a beautiful place didn't seem very important because life was so good there. Also, many of us Islanders didn't make a lot of money or have a lot of time to travel. However, I met my former husband in 1991 in P.E.I. In 1994, we travelled to Calgary, Alberta to be a part of my sister's wedding. We loved what Calgary had to offer (small town–big city feel and jobs) so much that we married in P.E.I. in 1995 and drove across the country to live in Calgary.

Sandra, meanwhile, had found the love of her life, Allison, during junior high at Stella Maris School in North Rustico. She married Allison, and they stayed in P.E.I. (almost 5,000 km from me in Calgary) and raised two amazing young men. Sandra had never really travelled far from P.E.I.; life was busy raising kids, and her husband was often away for work.

Well, the PLD course always presented opportunities for me to step up. I reconnected with Sandra because I realized that she is a very important person in my life, and I need to step up and let her know. I was learning to let people know how much I love and care for them today (and not wait for another day to go by). This was an important understanding that was becoming more apparent to me.

I called her one day and asked if she would be interested in taking a trip to see me in Calgary. I had been back to P.E.I. many, many times and always saw Sandra when I travelled back home (of course, these were all family trips). At the time, I didn't realize it was such a big ask. I didn't realize how monumental this was going to be for her. You see, she had never been on a plane or a big trip by herself. I was so freakin' excited for this opportunity for her! I was so privileged to be part of this for her.

After discussing dates and what worked best for me (as I was still working), I booked her flight. Her hubby set her up with an understanding of where she was going in the airport (as she had one stopover) and set her up for success.

I was truly blessed and excited to have her arrive at the Calgary airport. I had even gotten my Grade 1 & 2 students excited. They made her a "Welcome to Calgary" sign, and she was tickled pink when Scott and I shared it with her at the airport.

Best friend Sandra arriving in Calgary

Wow! What a blessing to have my BFF there and meet the beautiful man that came into my life (in person). Over the week of her stay, Scott hung out with her during the day, and I took some time off to take her to some tourist spots, like Banff to ride the gondola and an afternoon dessert 626 ft (190.8 m) up in the Calgary tower and step onto the glass floor. I later learned that those two events in themselves were big, as Sandra had a slight fear of heights.

April 2022

I thought it would be cool if Sandra and Scott volunteered in my classroom to support my students in making puppets. They both agreed when I asked. Well, look at that—I was being confident and asking for what I wanted. Okay. I'm proud of myself!

My students were super excited to have both Sandra and Scott in the classroom. They loved having volunteers help us out, as this was pretty novel for these young kids who didn't see much of it because of Covid restrictions over the past year or so. Can you believe I got my best childhood friend and the big, Harley-riding, tattooed sleeves guy who didn't have much success and happiness in school volunteering in my Grade 1 & 2 class? Well, the kids loved Sandra and Scott. And, of course, they enjoyed having two extra sets of hands helping them make paper puppets.

During the last few days of Sandra being in Calgary, I noticed she didn't have a nose ring as I remember she used to have. So, I asked her about it. Apparently, she had taken it out during the Covid pandemic. Because it was difficult to get out and make appointments, she let it grow over. I asked her if she would like to just get her nose piercing redone in Calgary and that I would like to get one at the same time with her.

You see, I've been starting to do things that I thought for most of my life were risks or unnecessary things for me to do. For example, back in 2018, my daughter and I went to get tattoos together. Brianna approached me with this idea, and I am so glad I had said yes to her. We both got a similar tattoo that she designed, and I will have that memory forever. Here was another opportunity for a new experience. Sandra and I booked an appointment, and it was great to feel supported by someone who has done it before. I got my little diamond piercing on the right side of my nose, and she on her left. I sure do appreciate the time spent with the people who mean the most to me.

Little did I realize it would affect how Scott and I kissed for the next month or so, as it was in the healing process (and still somewhat affects the way we kissed over a year later). We got caught on it a few times and, oh, it hurt for both of us. He didn't overly love it for that fact; however, he knew I wanted it, and we managed to still get in as many kisses as possible.

It was a gift having Sandra come to spend time in Calgary. I am slowly learning that the important people in my life need to know they are important to me through my actions and words.

I live for today; if tomorrow never comes, they will know how much I care and love them.

CHAPTER 10

May 2022

Saying Goodbye

It was the first of May, my school schedule was very busy, and we were getting ready for the big gala. Life was zooming along. I was just approved last month for my leave of absence from the Calgary Board of Education as we were planning our trip to Thailand. I was biting at the bit to apply for our travel visa, which could only be applied for three months before leaving (we initially planned to go at the end of August, then later moved to the end of September, as we had another personal development course we signed up to in New Mexico).

I was on an emotional rollercoaster, believing that I would be leaving the school I was at for fourteen years; saying goodbye to the staff I was working with and have come to be great friends with; and not being able to say a proper goodbye to my students at the end of the school year, as I had planned to attend a Women's Leadership course in New Mexico during my last week of work.

I started my goodbyes during one of my Moving and Munching sessions, where once a month I'd invite family members to join us for a workout to a few songs chosen by my students, then we'd eat some veggies and have a little social. I chose to be brave at the end when everyone was chewing on their veggies. I told everyone how I planned to take a year off work from the Calgary Board of Education and that I was going to Thailand with my boyfriend, Scott (yet to be married at this point).

That was a big risk in my world. Often in a small school, students will know (or have a good idea) which teacher they will have the following year. In my school, we often looped students. For a few years, we let students know during the summer who their teacher would be; each teacher would write a postcard to their students for the upcoming year and welcome them to their class. If I had a student in Grade 1, then I could have them again in Grade 2; we often had multi-grade classrooms due to smaller numbers in the school, which allowed for multi-aging and more choice to move students around if need be.

Before I revealed my plans, several parents and students had told me how they're excited to have me as their teacher the following year. I loved their level of appreciation.

I was proud of myself for being brave that day. I did not even have plans for where we would live, whether I would teach there, where I wanted to explore, and so on. Scott and I were really just jumping in and just doing it. (JFDI!)

I learned a lesson that day. I can share anything, even when I don't know all the answers. I am really learning to be brave and have confidence in myself when I speak. I've come far with this blockage in my head. For most of my life, I did not share my thoughts and opinions very much because I either don't remember information, (history or geography) or don't think that what I have to share is important or interesting. I've talked myself into thinking that I would look dumb or stupid.

I've come to an understanding that if I talk and share and not know exactly what I'd say, I usually get my point across. Being open and honest about not remembering information is okay. That's me, and that's okay.

Mother's Day

May was also the month of Mother's Day. I wanted this Mother's Day to be special, one to remember. So, about a month prior, I asked my two children if they would want to go together to get a tattoo for Mother's Day. Both my children already had tattoos and knew that having Mom splurge on them and get a tattoo would be something they would appreciate. I told them this was my gift to them, as I was going away to Thailand for six months. More importantly, I have realized that time spent together is what is important. A win-win! So, the kids planned their tattoos (of course, with a budget in mind), and we set off to the tattoo artists' house.

We were introduced to Matthew, the tattoo artist, via another friend I had met through my personal development work. Matthew had previously worked in a tattoo shop and now works at home. Jordan decided on two small tattoos—a bee with a knife and some cartoon character ghost guy. As for Brianna, she had just purchased a live ball python snake, so her tattoo was a replica of it wrapped around a flower on her arm. For me, I knew I wanted something special too.

As I mentioned, Brianna and I went for tattoos together a few years back. Now I wanted to add to that tattoo. I was with Scott, and I knew I wanted something that had a connection to him.

Back in January, when I was finally leaving Mexico after my extended Covid stay, I wanted to pick up some sort of item to remember my time with Scott or my experience of being there by myself. I found myself in the jewellery store at the airport. There was the perfect item—a silver bracelet with a heart intertwined with the infinity symbol. I have worn it every day since then. It symbolizes the love I will forever have for Scott. I thought I could use these two symbols (the heart and the infinity) for my tattoo.

When I showed Matthew, we had a hard time arranging the heart and infinity symbol with the previous tattoo I had gotten with Brianna. So, Matthew recommended two hearts intertwined—PERFECT!

I know what you might be thinking: "Don't you know you should not get your boyfriend tattooed on your body? What if you break up?" Well, I knew what to do. You are right; I did not want to put names on my body. It was about the symbols. My love for Scott will never change. I have told him on many occasions that his love has impacted my life so greatly that if I ever lost him, he has forever changed my heart for the better. His love has so impacted me that this tattoo was to say that. My heart is forever intertwined with his, so the joining of the two hearts as my tattoo would be it.

You may be wondering why Scott was not joining us to get tattoos, as he has the most tattoos of all of us! He was actually away that weekend, and that was okay. The kids and I had a blast, and it was about us spending time together and creating those memories that I know I will cherish forever. And, of course, we love our tattoos. Also, Scott wants a larger tattoo to cover his back or one of his best Jack Russell dogs, Tymer.

Let me tell you, tattoos were *never* really considered in my old life. They seemed a little dumb to me. Why spend money writing on yourself? Why put permanent ink there when you might change your mind in a few years and don't like it? Well, that's where my mind has made some shifts. Life is too short. The first tattoo I got when I went with Brianna was the one of my children's birthdates. These two days were very monumental in my life. The birth and life of my two children has forever changed my life and brought more love into it. More importantly, it was about the time I got to spend with Brianna and Jordan and how much I will cherish that memory.

As I look down at the tattoo I had gotten of my kids' birthdates, I need to tell you an interesting story about my son's birthday too. When I first met Scott and we were getting to know each other, of course, we discussed when our birthdays were. How ironic was it that Scott's birthday is the same date and month as my son's? So, can I say that, technically, I already had Scott tattooed on me before even meeting him? Sure. Ha ha!

The tattoo with the intertwined hearts represents the work I have done in revealing more of the person I have always had deep inside me. I am the person who is now starting to really show up in my life. I have no regrets about getting any of these tattoos, and I'm so proud for stepping out and making decisions for myself and what I want.

The Gala Night

It was the night of our PLD gala. Scott drove me (and my garment bag filled with secretly packed outfits; I planned to do some dress changes as the night went along) to the hotel where the gala was being held and went back home to prepare for the night. I met up with Julie, a friend we met through our personal development work, to get our hair and make-up done together.

When I met up with Julie at the hotel, she was practicing some karaoke songs in her room. You see, Julie loved doing karaoke and took pride in her singing skills. We enjoyed her mastery of such a skill. When we got our hair and make-up done, I noticed that the make-up artist was caking on the make-up well beyond my typical liking. Right away, I was starting to get creases of make-up on my face and was uncomfortable with how thick and dark the make-up artist was shading my eyebrows. That look is definitely not for me, that's for sure.

So, I was assertive when I saw how my make-up was looking. I looked fear in the face and spoke up about my make-up. I was proud that I was showing up as a more confident person. When I moved on to get my hair done, I approached the hairdresser with clarity about the way I wanted my hair to look—hair on my shoulders, sides pulled back, simple and pretty. I am proud of myself for growing in this area and choosing to be heard.

Let the night, which I was remaining open to, begin!

As I said, Scott had gone back home and got ready in his tux. He drove down to the hotel to meet us. He was all dapper in his black tuxedo and riding on his bright orange Street Glide Harley-Davidson— quite a statement, if I do say so myself. He wasn't overly excited about wearing the red bowtie with his tux, as he loved to wear the white tie to match the white Converse sneakers. However, I wanted him to match me and my cherry red dress.

Scott on Gala night

We met up with Tomas, another friend from our ninety-day course and the seven-day Ranch experience, before the big evening for a quick snack and drink in the hotel bar. Some snacks, water and coffee got us ready for the evening. I felt like a beauty queen in that dress. Got lots of wows and curious stares as the cherry red lace train trailed well behind me as I walked.

The PLD group met in the hallways and later convened in a room for pictures of various types—whole group, guys, girls, couples. We quenched our thirst with cold water, and Scott wore his crown. It was a little uncomfortable. However, I looked beyond it and remained open. I focussed my attention on others and on connecting with them. A few other group members came in with novelty suits, which lightened up the evening and the strain of how Scott's crown may be taken. No one questioned the crown or overly noticed it (as far as I was aware).

That put my mind at ease, and I thought that my stance of remaining open to the evening let it become what I hoped it might be—a night of celebration and fun. I knew my mindset was what was making this evening run smoothly. I chose to remain open, so the night was a wonderful celebration.

My beautiful dress was complimented by many. I was proud to stand by my man, who was very handsome in his tux. However, why not mix it up a little?

I'm not sure where I got the idea; however, I know my interest in showing up for my man was important to me. That night, I decided that this beautiful gown may be too much to wear all evening and dance in later. So, I made a plan, as a surprise for Scott and fun for me!

When the dinner and acknowledgements were all done, and it was time to let loose and shake our booties on the dance floor, it was time to begin the dress-change plan. I spoke with Julie earlier about going back up to her room to do a dress change. So, we headed up to her hotel room. I changed into a black cocktail dress and kept on the red suede pumps. It was fun and pretty cute. Scott loved the change, and we danced for an hour or so.

Scott suffered a lot of physical pain—neck pain, back pain and just overall physical pain—so dancing isn't always his thing because of it. However, he endured it, and we had a blast dancing together and with friends. To keep him interested (and maybe help him fight through the pain), I told him I would be back and he could sit down and take a break. It was time for the third dress of the night. I connected with Julie again, and we headed back to her room.

I re-entered the dance floor, and Scott knew I was a brave and proud woman. I wore a body-hugging, short, black dress and my black Under Armour sneakers to continue having more fun with my man on the dance floor. By this time, the dance floor was hopping, and the night was getting late (for us old timers—ha ha). I strutted my stuff because I was happy. I was confident. Life could not be any better. That little number of a dress was the icing on the cake for the evening. Maybe for Scott, a little relief for the pain.

What a gala night we had! We still talk about the three-dress changes and that one decision helped make that night a great night. The old me would not take risks like this out of fear of failure or that it wouldn't be fun enough or work out how I thought. I'm so glad I now live with some risk in my life, ride the waves of both success and failure, take opportunities for growth, and find new awareness of myself. I am extremely proud of my own personal growth this year. The fact that Scott sees my growth and inspires me to continue to grow is something I know I deserve in my life.

With an Unfortunate Event Comes Gratitude

Not only did I attend a gala this month and get tattoos with my kids, but I was also so super pumped because my mom planned a trip to Calgary to see my sister and me! I have not physically seen my mom since before Covid, the summer of 2019. That's too long not to hold your mom in your arms.

My mom arrived at the airport. Scott and I, along with my sister, greeted her. She came in with one of her best friends from P.E.I. and, at the same time, got to catch up with Mom's best friend's son, who also lives about an hour away from Calgary and was picking her up.

I was so excited to have my mom here. She has been impactful in my life. She was my Kindergarten teacher when I was five years old. Everybody loved my mom. Many, many parents beamed when they knew their child would have my mom as a teacher. She was loving, patient and always taught with a positive attitude. Gee, do you think that's where I got my style of teaching from?

Mom's first night in Calgary

Mom stayed at my sister's house first and then was scheduled to come over to my house several days later. This was Mom's first time meeting Scott, in person that is. We had many Skype calls together, although none as funny as the "sorry jar" one! I think my mom felt Scott's love when he embraced her for the first time. I know she knows I am happy with Scott and he's who I want to be with.

This place of excitement turned fairly quickly when, within twelve hours or so, I got a WhatsApp message from my sister saying that Mom had fallen and that they were waiting for an ambulance to arrive. Lana took Mom out to see her work at the Calgary Police Service, and Mom fell as she was walking down the curb from the sidewalk. To make a long story short, Mom broke her elbow and hit her leg and ribs, which made them quite tender. She got elbow surgery in Calgary within a week, which was great news. So, what was going to be a few-weeks trip to Calgary turned into a six-week stay.

My sister looked after my mom most of the time during her recovery, as she mostly worked from home and I worked at school five days a week. Although Scott was home, we also had two dogs in the house and there was some concern that they could easily knock Mom over or be under her feet and make her trip. By the last week or so of her recovery, Mom made her way over to our house. Scott assured me he would keep the dogs away from Mom and give her the attention and care she needed.

Mom spent several days at our house and rested during the day with Scott. Scott learned what she liked for breakfast and lunch. He made sure to ask her about her needs, like another cup of hot water and snacks during the day. It may have been awkward, as she was now hanging out with this "strange man" (technically). She had only just met him in person on a few occasions at this point and was now relying on him to feed her and keep her safe from the dogs in the house. You see, the dogs were a busy little fifteen-pound Jack Russel, Norton, and a fairly calm, white furry eighty-pound Great Pyrenees mix, Alya. When you have a 78-year-old mom recovering from elbow surgery, you don't need dogs tripping her up. I was 100 percent confident that Scott would keep his word and look after her to the best of his ability. And, of course, he did. Mom and Scott got to know each other a little more, and I think that was a good thing.

I was sad to see my mom go back home. I was so blessed to have had her come to Calgary and be able to hold her in my arms again. With the unfortunate event of breaking her elbow came more gratitude. I was able to see her for a longer period, and Scott had the opportunity to hang out with her. This extended stay also allowed her and my sister more time to connect. I also appreciated the responsibility Lana took with Mom's care and appointments at the beginning of her healing—something I could not have dedicated myself to as she did. All great blessings and so much gratitude.

I also was reminded that my mom is so precious to me. Even though we've connected over the past several years via Skype, when you get to hold your mom in your arms, you realize she isn't young anymore and having that time with her is so precious. It truly is important to make sure the people in your life know how much you love and care for them.

Back at the Ranch

If there wasn't enough awesomeness already happening in May, we still had more. We were hosting Scott's friend, Mike, and niece, Tara. Mike drove to Calgary from Kamloops, and Tara flew in from Toronto. Scott had offered both of them the initial three-day weekend to work on their own personal growth. Now they were on the next step—the Ranch. This was the same place Scott and I met and fell in love.

Having Mike and Tara at the house gave me a glimpse into how Scott was with his friends and family. I had the opportunity to see that when Scott believed in someone, it touched his core and theirs.

Mike has been Scott's buddy for decades, and Scott truly believed in wanting the best for his buddy. I believe Mike saw the benefits from doing his own PD work and the similar background in Alcoholics Anonymous (AA), Scott was stoked for Mike and the opportunity for growth from this week-long experience.

Scott also shared with me how he wanted to positively impact his niece Tara's life. Scott's connection with his family has been hindered over the years. But now, with his renewed sense of well-being, he finds himself reaching out to those who are receptive. Tara is one of those family members who see Scott for the great man he is and is receptive to him and the growth he has had in his life.

At the end of Mike and Tara's Ranch experience, Scott and I made our way there to surprise them on their graduation night. They both appreciated our gesture of being there and acknowledging the work they put into themselves. It is also so rewarding to see how much Scott cares for his friends and family. He knows exactly what to say and can express his emotions, so others really feel him.

Scott's ability to express himself and be vulnerable in the moment is something I admired. At the beginning of our relationship, I often saw him as better than me in this area. And really, he was. As he explained to me, "Lisa, I've had to stand in front of many AA meetings and share. I've had lots of opportunities."

That was true, and I knew I was on my way to re-learning how to show more emotions and be vulnerable when I speak. I have improved over the time I have known him. I still continue to strive for more from myself. I know I will get there; I just need to be gentle to myself.

The celebration of seeing friends and family glow more after that one week is so rewarding. And I also had something else in mind for that night. This was *the* spot Scott and I first met less than a year earlier. I had to do something, right?

I excitedly pulled Tara aside and said, "I need your help." I know what you're thinking: Where did this confident Lisa come from?

I picked up my purse, and we went to the washroom, and I told her my plan. She was excited.

She went out front and told Scott I needed him in the washroom. She escorted him to the washroom and yelled in that Scott was there and that I could come out now.

I walked out with that butterfly dress I know he loved seeing me in, the one I wore the night we graduated from our week at the Ranch just under a year ago. Again, I know Scott appreciated that little surprise. Even better, I showed Tara how much I appreciate her uncle and how important he is to me that I will do fun things, like a dress change, all in the name of love.

Wearing the butterfly dress, almost one year later

When Mike and Tara were in Calgary, we also took the time to go for a ride—of course! Mike had ridden his Harley to Calgary from Kamloops, and Tara borrowed Scott's green Dyna—the one I had first ridden on with Scott back when I first met him. Oh, the great memories.

The Perfect Ring

Scott and I knew early in our relationship that we would marry someday; we were just not sure exactly when. We actually looked at an engagement ring and wedding band for me back in December before going to Mexico. I put on several different styles of rings; however, nothing spoke to me. I knew I wanted white gold and nothing too gaudy or blingy. I never thought of myself as wanting anything too *show-offish* or flashy. I knew what I didn't want . . . but what was I wanting?

We were in the South Center Mall in Calgary one day and decided to check out rings at the jewellery store. I remained open that I would find exactly what I was looking for. Well, I did. It was a princess ring—a square cut with a larger diamond in the middle, surrounded by smaller diamonds. Both the engagement ring and wedding band were also set with diamonds. It was perfect!

Found the perfect ring

I did have a few challenges with the ring, that I was determined to find a solution. I think the challenges were with my finger. However, finger surgery was not on the list of solutions. You see, my knuckles were a little big, which meant that when I got the ring on, it rotated and rotated constantly.

The customer sales rep helping us suggested that along with a slight size reduction, they can also square off the bottom of each band to reduce rotation. We got that done, but it only helped a little bit. The engagement ring still spun around and around. I did find another temporary solution: a plastic piece to slide under the ring. That works, for sure; however, that plastic piece got dirty and wore out over time.

I was reassured that when I got married and the band and engagement ring were together on my finger, they would rotate less. I knew I also wanted to solder them together, which may improve my problem. However, I was bound and determined to find my solution because that was that. I loved the rings; they spoke to me the day I found them.

As for Scott, he wanted a yellow gold ring. When we were discussing what kind of ring Scott wanted to get, he scared me a bit. He was excited to tell me about the ring he had for his first marriage. It was a collection of skulls. He no longer had that ring, and he would look for another cool idea. We looked at several styles, and he never gravitated towards a skull ring—yeah! Okay, okay. I was actually open to whatever he really wanted. The choice he did end up picking was really cool.

Scott was in Vancouver when he found his ring. He found a yellow gold ring with loops like a gold chain. He was attending a personal development course where some of his friends were graduating from. He took a picture and asked me what I thought. I thought it was really neat, and I knew he picked it and liked it. That was what was important.

We finally had our rings picked, and we were well on our way to marrying each other at some point. We were so busy at that point, we had not discussed any specific day for a wedding. We knew it would come, and we would be ready when the time was right.

CHAPTER 11

June 2022

Ride Through the Fear

It was finally June. As a teacher, it was a crazy time of year—wrapping up students' report cards, finalizing the year, school planning for next year, and kids are just done. Summer is coming.

Scott challenged me early on in our relationship to take motorcycle lessons. As part of expanding my life, taking on challenges is something I'm taking in stride. I thought I could handle this challenge, no problem. This month, I've planned two weekends of about six hours each day for a Too Cool Motorcycle School course. The instructors were amazing, positive, fun, and they always had a corny joke to go along with whatever skill we were learning.

Throughout the four classes, I had moments of feeling successful and other moments where tears welled up (fortunately, I had a full-face helmet to hide some of the tears). I initially walked into this motorcycle school thinking, *I got this!* I know how to drive a standard car. I know how to shift. I know how gears work. I got this! Well, a motorcycle is quite different.

I never spoke of the challenges I had years ago with my left side arm and leg. I was having weird spasms in my left hand and foot. They were getting so bad that, at one point, I took myself to a hospital, wondering if I was having a stroke. They confirmed with a hard NO that it was not a stroke. *Whew,* I thought.

However, what was it? I even took time off a school start-up a few years ago because I was not sleeping and could not operate with these left-side spasm and pain. I took off about a month from work to focus on my body, gain strength and get some level of sleep to operate during the day.

Within a year of this medical leave from work, I had told my former husband I needed to move on from our relationship of twenty-five years. At that point, I started to feel more relief from my left-side body pain. I would not say all my pain stemmed from how I operated in our relationship; however, I now know in my heart that my choice to move forward in my life was part of the stress my body was showing.

The left side of my body was definitely not letting me feel like I was in full control of operating a motorcycle—at least, that is what my brain was telling me. I'm sure the stress of being a struggling student also triggered my left-side symptoms. I struggled with learning a new skill, just like I did with the scuba diving lessons. I was ready to quit on more than one occasion during the four long days of classes. However, I needed to remember (and was often reminded) to be "gentle on myself." Yes, here it was again—learning a new skill and feeling too dumb and stupid to get it quick enough. Again, like the scuba diving lessons, I felt like I was behind Scott in a skill.

At this point, I met another friend of Scott's—Lori, a Harley rider herself. She assured me to be patient and check out some videos that would help me with my skills. I later met other ladies who were Harley riders, and they, too, said in their own words what Scott always reminds me, "Be gentle on yourself."

In the last few hours of the fourth day of classes, the instructor described how we would drive around Calgary on a pre-set destination, and we were told we would be getting on the highway. For some reason, I didn't compute the word *highway* with the fact that I (little old beginner rider *me*!) would ride on two wheels at 100 km/h. However, that's what I did! AHHHHHH! I rode a motorcycle at 100 km/h (for a portion of the time), and I had only had three full days of practice under my belt.

Were they (motorcycle instructors) crazy to let such a brand-new driver do this? However, I did it. And that's all I can say! Breaking new personal walls and barriers! Going through the fear. Being confident.

This class was only meant for riders to gain more experience and learn the proper motorcycle skills and etiquette. I have yet to pass a road test on a motorcycle and earn a provincial licence to ride (not drive) a motorcycle. That's the next challenge if I wish to pursue it!

Practicing shifting when not on a bike.

All this work I was doing on myself was stretching my ability to be patient with myself, to celebrate that I was walking through fears and challenges. I am fortunate to be reminded by Scott to celebrate how brave I am to be stepping forward into my life. I was smashing misbeliefs about myself left and right.

Women's Workshop

I flew to Albuquerque, New Mexico for a women's-only course. Yes, more personal development. Again, at a ranch with no cell reception, where seventy other women and I were challenged to grow, expand our abilities and become a better version of ourselves.

I participated in challenges, like becoming a better communicator and understanding that communication is a huge part of my learning.

So, I continued to be open to the possibility that clear communication and being brave to communicate is still an area of growth for me. I kept thinking of this mantra I chose when I was on a recent course with my beautiful husband, "I trust myself and always contribute what I have to give (in every situation)."

This is big for me, as being the quiet one and not saying a word is the way I've lived my life. Sitting on the fence and not having an opinion has also been my stance. Sharing without worry or fear has been a big challenge for me in my life. However, I continue to take risks and practice being brave and speaking up.

After this week at the women's course, I understood that I do not stand alone in my thoughts and worries about how I operate in this world. Throughout the week, many other women shared and communicated their doubts and fears too. I was grateful to be with a group of women who talked openly about it and supported each other in their journey of growth.

On a daily basis, Scott reminds me of how brave we both are in what we strive to become and who we want to be in this world. If you, yourself, do not have that partner supporting you in this type of growth, like I am fortunate to have, then having other like-minded people you can reach out to and support you is necessary.

During the women's course. I had found the courage to stand up in front of these seventy women to share a little about myself. I introduced myself as Lisa Maze (at that point, still not married to my Mr. Brearley) and needed everyone's support in workshopping my divorce papers in my mailbox, as I had just submitted those papers back in March and was told they would take a few months to process. During this course, I needed the group of ladies to really see my divorce papers in that super mailbox across the road from our house.

Workshopping, as I requested the group to do, is a mindset I learned, which basically means using positive thinking and visualization to see what you need or want.

I bravely, and nervously, requested everyone to workshop those divorce papers in the super mailbox across the street in front of my house. I, too, believed they were there. Again, I was seeing myself take small steps in building my confidence in sharing what I needed.

Women's Leadership Course in Albuquerque, New Mexico

After the week on the course, I stayed at a hotel in New Mexico for the night before my flight back to Canada. As soon as I connected to the hotel's Wi-Fi, Scott and I were on our first video call after a week of missing him. He said he had something to show me. He sent a picture of the envelope wherein the divorce papers were, which meant the workshopping from all those women worked and there's one less bump in the road on our way to our beautiful wedding day (whenever that would be).

After a few minutes of chatting, we both had a similar thought almost simultaneously. You see, Scott took advantage of the fact that I was away at a week-long course to drive down into the States and pick up car parts for the Dodge Dart he was getting restored. We had not planned it, but when we talked, we both thought about changing my flight from going straight back home to Canada to rerouting my flight to meet him in Spokane, Washington. We could drive back home together. Brilliant!

It was a great plan, and I have been open to this type of flexibility all my life. That was something I liked about Scott too; I appreciate how he can live in the moment and be flexible. I was so excited to see Scott again and hold him and kiss him after a week with a bunch of ladies. No offence, ladies—love you all!

Scott's Family

When I arrived in Spokane, Scott picked me up at the airport in my Rav4, which he drove to pick up the car parts with. I remember thinking it's weird seeing him in that car—of course, not his first choice of wheels (coming from the big-ass truck and motorcycle world!).

Anyway, I was so excited to finally hold him again and even more excited to meet some of his family. I was about to meet his Aunt Cathy, Scott's mom's sister. Remember the mom he doesn't communicate with and I've never spoken to or met yet? So, it was great to meet some of Scott's family with whom he had good relations and see that side of his life.

Scott had spoken fondly of his Aunt Cathy and had some good memories of her when he was younger. He has kept in contact with her over the years. I got to meet and hang out with two of his little cousins, who were staying with their Aunt Cathy at the time. I got to see a playful side of Scott that I rarely saw. Fun Uncle Scott played with the two boys at a trampoline park. Even with the possibility of physically "hurting" himself, he had a blast with the boys. It was a beautiful sight to watch and be a part of.

I was learning more about this wonderful man and seeing how the man I am with today was moulded by those past experiences and people in his life. At that point, I only knew that he did not really associate with any of his family because of his past experiences. What I came to learn about him was that he was choosing to move forward and have only positive people in his life.

I have always supported Scott in how he connects with those family members he feels will look at him positively and recognize he is making every effort to move forward in his life. I love you, babe, and I will continue to do my best in making those forward-walking choices with you.

CHAPTER 12

July 2022

One Table Full

When I arrived back from the Women's Leadership course, school was all out and done for another year. However, I never truly cleaned out my classroom for the new teacher to take over. I was at the school with the summer cleaners, and I invited my daughter to help me get things organized, sorted and pared down, so I didn't have to transport too much stuff up to Ashcroft, B.C.

You see, we decided that I would head up to Ashcroft with Scott, and we would rent out my house in Calgary when we move to Thailand. I set my mind to getting rid of years and years of teacher stuff, which can get pretty daunting.

What weighs heavy on this teacher's mind in this sort of purging is, "What will I be teaching next year, and will I use this again?"

As I was clearing out my classroom, I pondered long and hard about all the changes I went through—my divorce, my new relationship, my plan to travel and explore Southeast Asia, becoming certified to scuba dive, taking motorcycle-riding lessons and endless amounts of new understandings and awareness about myself. It has been a mind-blowing year!

I was feeling more confident to say that I was a smart, creative and more confident woman. Whatever I needed in the future, I would find it. It would come my way. At that point, I was questioning if I even wanted to come back to work as a full-time teacher. I saw new opportunities for me, and I was at a point in my life to take on new adventures. Even though my future did not have a clear and simple plan (like work until I retire as a teacher), I knew I had the capabilities to be open and move towards new and exciting new adventures for me.

So, Brianna and I ended up with one table full of teacher supplies that I was taking to my new home in Ashcroft, B.C. It was stacked a few levels high, though it was only one table full.

Will This Wedding Happen?

During the first week of July, Scott decided to do some volunteer work for the Personal Development business we've been on our journey with over the past few years. On his own time and dime, he flew to Toronto, Ontario and staffed a three-day weekend course of personal development. Giving back in this way is essential to him. He inspires me with his drive to do so and how giving back enriches his life.

I absolutely love how he shared with me one significant learning from this volunteer weekend. He learned he had more compassion than he ever thought he had. This beautiful understanding is what I love about Scott and our relationship. Scott is so open to sharing his thoughts and real feelings regarding his own personal awareness of his growth. I find this so attractive. It was on my list of "requirements" of a man, a partner, a soulmate and a lover.

I still find myself almost speechless some days and, in some ways, overwhelmed with the overload of words about how I feel about this extraordinary man. Scott is truly a special soul, and I know I deserve him. However, over our year, I second-guessed this. I often saw myself as "not a great catch." I had a lot of self-doubt and did not feel I was always worthy of such a great man in my life. To this day, I feel I must have manifested him into my life. I must have known I was ready to meet him.

Anyway, when Scott was doing this volunteer work in Toronto, he and everyone else who volunteered made it a priority to make a thirty-day goal. Goals are important in this work of personal development. Scott was honest and initially said he wasn't sure what his goal would be. Then it came to him—MARRY LISA!

When he shared this with other volunteers, they questioned him. "Are you sure? Do you need to ask Lisa first?"

You see, we talked about marriage very early on in our relationship. We knew we were 100 percent committed, and marriage was another step in our relationship. I had no questions about marrying Scott. When I met him, I was sure I was going to get to know this guy a lot more. As I did, I knew I wanted him in my life. I had no uncertainties about him.

Scott called me from Toronto and shared his goal with me. I was a little surprised. However, I knew that the feeling I was having was also connected to me being scared or hesitant to take risks in life. The moment he finished telling me his goal, I immediately went to my past feeling about fear—the fear that I wouldn't be capable of planning a wedding in thirty days! How would I organize and plan a wedding in thirty days? Really? Could I actually do this and have what I wanted for our wedding? How did I want this day to be? Who did I want to be there? With such short notice, who would show up?

All these thoughts raced through my mind, along with the fear of planning a wedding in thirty days. Yet, the certainty of who I was marrying far outweighed the scariness of planning it all. I've also come to realize that Lisa is a much more confident woman who can make bold decisions in her life. So, bring it on!

I was marrying the man I loved with every ounce of my being, and I looked forward to being married to him. I knew, in my gut, that this man had so much love to give, and I was worthy of it all. I knew I wanted to explore life and meet challenges with him. I knew that I was so moved and was greatly influenced by how he has shown up in my life that I was open to more of that. With that understanding, we were well on our way to planning a wedding in thirty days!

While Scott was still in Toronto, I had time to think more about our wedding. I knew I wanted to get him something special for our day. However, what was the "perfect" gift? He wasn't big on trinkets and there wasn't a lot of time to get something extra special made, but I knew he would appreciate whatever I got him. It is interesting when you open your mind to any possibilities, good things come your way.

I was scrolling through Facebook one day, and (almost like out of nowhere) there was a post of this lady playing a song for her husband.

You see, she had a song specially made for him. She recorded him hearing it for the first time while driving in the car. His look of surprise at how the words were all about how she felt about him—it was moving and got me all warm inside.

Over the next few days, more and more ads like this came up. I took note of the website that was linked to writing and creating your own song—Song Finch. I thought that this could be perfect! I logged onto Song Finch, and before long, I answered all the questions about how we met and how we were 100 percent committed to each other. Shazam! The song was made. Actually, I had to wait a week for it to be completed. However, the idea was, "Shazam! Done." I found the perfect gift.

Scott was still in Toronto, and our big day was just under two weeks away. Song Finch said the completed song would be emailed to me within a week or so. When it had finally arrived in my inbox, I sat by myself in my kitchen, listening to the song.

I started to cry.

This was a perfect gift. The singer was great, and the song was called "It All Pointed to You." I decided to play this song for our first dance after our official wedding ceremony. Yes, you heard me. I decided, and it was a surprise to Scott.

Making decisions, like finding the gift or deciding to have a first dance and choosing the song, was not something I typically felt confident about throughout most of my life. Scott had no idea about this song or the first dance. I confidently made that decision and went with my gut. I'm so glad that my level of bravery and confidence is slowly becoming more of the person I want to be or the person I am slowly rediscovering.

Even if playing this perfect song didn't work out (for whatever reason), I would have been disappointed; however, I have learned over this year to get over disappointments much more quickly. I have learned to take more "little" risks like this and be okay with what happens. I have learned not to beat myself up over them and just move on. Scott and I have noticed that this is an area of personal growth that has improved over this year for both of us.

Anyway, Scott was still in Toronto, and it was up to me to get a move on planning the wedding. There was no time to wait. First things first, we needed someone to marry us!

With the personal development group that we were associated with, I thought there *must* be someone out there who could marry us. I thought that the people we've grown to know over the past few years would know someone who could marry us and be excited and flexible in helping us make this "quickly organized" day happen. We also decided on two possible dates (around July 16 or July 23). We were scrounging a bit to find the best Justice of the Peace to marry us in the backyard of our Calgary home. The date we choose may have to depend on the Justice of the Peace's availability, as we were pretty late in requesting one.

I went to Facebook (where else these days?) to put out the request to my FB friends, and heard back from Andre Lam. I had the pleasure of meeting Mr. Lam during our PLD course, where Scott and I planned that online presentation for anyone interested in this personal development work. Mr. Lam was our main speaker for the online event. I truly love how he confidently shared the message of how personal development can shift your life.

Andre got back to me indicating that he knew someone—Rene Pierno. He sent her information to me, and I reached out to Rene on the phone. We hit it off when I spoke with her, and she was excited. I felt quite connected when we spoke, and I knew she was the right JP for us!

From my conversation with Rene on July 9, she told me she could feel how much I loved Scott and would be excited to celebrate our day. She and I were so excited about the wedding that we didn't even realize she was in Edmonton and I was in Calgary—a three-hour drive away from each other. When we figured out the distance, there was no concern. Rene said she would head down to Calgary in the late morning and arrive about an hour and a half to spare for the ceremony, as long as she could change her outfit when she arrived. We were both super excited!

Rene emailed the outline of the service she typically performs. I altered what I needed, and she was good with my choices. I asked Scott about the details, and he was happy with it too. With the date of July 23 chosen and the JP booked, our wedding was less than two weeks away.

The Roadblocks

From my conversation with Rene, we needed to get a marriage licence as soon as possible. Scott and I were both divorced at this point; mine very recent (remember workshopping the divorce papers in the super mailbox?) and Scott about eight years prior. Scott returned to Calgary from his goal-making course in Toronto on Monday, July 11. We got up early on Tuesday and needed to get things moving for this wedding. It was eleven days before the date we were getting married. I had already printed off the registrations for the marriage licence and filled it in with our information. With our divorce papers in a brown envelope and the marriage registration form filled out, off we rode to the Registry office for its opening time at 9 a.m.

We took our number and waited in line, taking the time to touch each other, hold hands, look at each other and give each other delicate kisses as others around us waited too. We were excited about our wedding plans moving forward and missed each other since Scott had just got back from Toronto after a week away.

At this point in our relationship, I truly loved the public display of affection, whether someone was looking or not. I have come to realize that any time I can hold his hand, touch his skin, kiss his lips, I'm a happy girl.

When our number was called, we made our way up to the counter and presented our paperwork. After a quick look, the young gentleman behind the plexiglass barrier said our paperwork would not suffice. It was not the correct divorce paperwork. The divorce paperwork we had in our hands was not the final paperwork. So, technically, we could not get our marriage licence that day.

WHAT? Holy crap! We were getting married in a week and a half, with the date we told all our friends and family, and we didn't have the correct paperwork? The JP is all organized and everything! OMG! What?

We were a little taken aback at this roadblock, and with the work we had done on ourselves, we knew we needed to be solution-oriented. So, what were our choices?

Scott quickly got on the phone with his former wife, Shannon, who, fortunately, was on great terms with Scott. She said she would make her way to the courts in British Columbia and get the proper final paperwork and FedEx them to us ASAP. To get them quickly, we were unable to do that in Alberta. So grateful for Shannon doing that for us!

For me, I quickly made my way to the courts in Calgary and picked up the proper final paperwork in short order (the fastest thing that happened so far in all of these divorce proceedings—a five-minute wait to get that final paperwork).

In the meantime, while Shannon was getting that final paperwork sorted out in B.C., there was still the most important part of our day that was not solved yet—the dress! I already had the red suede high-heels from the gala night where I did my three-dress change. However, I went back and forth about what kind of dress I was looking for. I didn't want to spend a tonne of money on something I was going to wear once (more than likely), and I wanted to find the perfect dress. I knew I would find it.

I went out shopping to Value Village again with my daughter. On this day, though, Brianna was tired from the shopping we did before we got to VV and stayed in the car. I told her I'd be as quick as I could and be right back out if I didn't see something right away.

I walked in the shop and went straight to the back, where I knew the dress section was. And there it was—the dress. It was a full-length, soft peach-coloured dress with a cascade of fine netting that dropped down from the waist and caressed the floor, and the top was adorned with peach-coloured sequins. Beautiful and elegant.

I took it off the rack and gave it a once-over for any major concerns—no rips, tears or stains, and it had a zipper that worked. As I pulled it over my head and gave it a once-over in the mirror, a lady walked by and commented, "Wow, that looks beautiful on you."

I had literally spent ten minutes entering and paying for the dress. I knew I had my perfect wedding dress. The only thing to do was clean it. When I arrived home, I took it upon myself to do that and let it hang dry. If that did not work, then I would get it to the dry cleaners. At this point, it was about a week before the wedding.

I very carefully washed it in the sink and hung it out on my back deck over the hammock swing. It turned out fabulous. Awesome!

Now I had only one problem about the dress that I needed to solve. Either I needed a special bra that would not be seen with the low-cut back or I would go braless or have taped-up boobs (which was something I have never done before). I had the dress—check. Now to solve what to do with the "girls"!

By the next Tuesday, we had all of our correct divorce papers in hand, and we found ourselves back at the marriage registry. We did it! We got the marriage licence—check!

Staying positive and thinking positively results in positive things happening.

The Magical Wedding Day

It was finally the big day. The day Scott and I were to marry. The day we knew would come from early on in our relationship. We were both sure about that.

Scott's friends (who have become my friends over this year)—Mike, Mark, Lori and Doug (a friend who drove twelve hours from Vancouver for our wedding)—all contributed by cleaning up the house and setting out food for our day. I always did my best to be clear with instructions and, at the same time, had trust in them that they would contribute to our day. I knew all of it was out of love.

July 2022

It has been an interesting journey with Scott in regard to friends. As I mentioned before, I appreciated how Scott truly cares for his friends. He doesn't hold back and often tells it like it is. Mike, Scott's best man, is a great guy and has known Scott for many years, stemming back to their AA days. They had some time apart over the years yet have mostly stayed in contact. After Mike took the three-day course and later the seven-day course, he and Scott seemed to have more opportunities to love and care for each other at another deeper level. I was excited to have Mike as Scott's best man at our wedding.

When I met Mark, he had moved into Scott's house around November 2021. Scott asked him to manage renting out his two properties in Ashcroft, in exchange for a decent place to stay. Mark agreed to the arrangement, and when Scott and I did go back to Ashcroft later in September 2022, Mark was at his house. The three of us living there together worked out just fine! We all get along quite well, and I appreciate Mark for the friendship we have now.

Like Mike, Scott knew Mark from AA. They have known each other for many years and have kept in contact. Both Mark and Mike are great guys, and I can see how the three of them are friends and how being there for true friends really resonates with them.

Later in August, these two gentlemen, Mark and Mike, both drove seven hours to Calgary to help Scott and I move up to Ashcroft. They dedicated their time and effort to help a true friend, and I'm privileged to now call them my friends too. Love you guys.

Scott, Mike, Mark and me

As my brain raced with a checklist of items on this beautiful wedding day, I reminded myself: Stay open, stay calm, stay centred.

Sometimes easier said than done. I was getting a bit consumed by the day and the list of things to accomplish.

I appreciate how Scott can read me and is aware of the stressful moments we are in. The day was starting to really stress me out—the house, the make-up, a shower, my hair and boob tape (yes, gotta tape those boobs up, as I never did find the "just right" bra and decided that bra-less is not my thing). Scott came to me late in the morning and said, "We are going for a ride."

All I could think was, *WHAT? What the hell? Throw on a helmet on my wedding day? Take the risk of being late or not at the house if someone showed up? What? Take a bike ride?*

I took a deep breath. First, I said "What?" as in, "Over my dead body, we are not going biking."

I took a deep breath again. I suggested we go at 1 p.m. and not 12 p.m. as he has suggested. Yes, I think I needed to get out and step out of the stress zone.

He was right. Scott is often right. For me, taking the initiative to be heard and saying I can manage to go at 1 p.m. put some control in my court. Doing this with him showed me and him that I can let go, refocus and that I hear him. Also, what do I really have to lose? Staying open paid off. It felt great to get out of my house and feel the wind in my hair. (Not really, I was wearing a helmet. But you know what I mean)

This year I've learned that I always need to be open to hear others. It's a practice I still work on as I still find myself finishing Scott's sentences or saying something about what I thought I heard him say. I continue to work on my listening skills—really listening. Repeating what's been said, so I know I've heard it correctly, can be helpful too. Life continues to be about reflecting and practicing what will support me in my relationships (with Scott or anyone).

Our wedding day was here, and the day was moving along! I had asked my sister, Lana, to be my maid of honour. I've looked up to her for many years. She had a baby early in her life and had to make difficult choices. She bravely decided to keep her child and raise him. She raised a wonderful son, Bruce, and later a daughter, Melissa. Both are successful adults, and Lana is a proud mama and grandma.

Lana took time from her daughter's university graduation dinner celebration to be part of my wedding day. I take this notion as her way of showing me love and support in my relationship with Scott, which she saw develop over the past year. Lana and I are fairly close. We talked a lot over the years about challenges with our relationships and relied on each other for a listening ear. Today she chose to be part of my very special day—a gesture of love I am truly grateful for.

It was time to get my dress on, and Lana was there to help, even with a sore wrist that's been bothering her for several months. She helped to get my dress on and helped me with the boob tape. We joked that the boob tape looked like hockey tape—and if you know Canada and my family, hockey is a very common topic that is easy to make good jokes about, whether it's hockey season or not.

About a week before the wedding, I asked Brianna to be my make-up artist for the day, and she kindly said yes. It was something I knew she excelled at, and she knew I loved a simple but pretty look and that I did not want to look like it was caked on.

When she arrived at the house, we sat down on the couch that was pushed aside to make room for when guests arrived. Brianna worked in the natural light that shone through the big front windows. She knew exactly what to do. I knew I could trust her. I always trusted her and her opinion.

Our beautiful friend Julie, whom I had got my hair and make-up done with at our PLD gala evening, came to town to be a part of our special day. She has some great tech skills and has helped us out on a few occasions, such as getting my printer to work at home. Besides her tech-savvy ways, she was also our music guru, and from her karaoke experience, she knew how to get some great playlists of music. Who better to ask organize the music and set up the speakers for our wedding day? Julie found and played the music for our special guests. I asked her if she could get the song ready (that I had made through Song Finch) for the first dance. She confidently got that all organized too. Amazing! I appreciate Julie for making the music portion of our day run so smoothly.

My son arrived shortly after Brianna and I started the make-up session. I was so excited to have both him and his beautiful girlfriend, Alannah, there for this special day. I asked Jordan to take the responsibility of carrying around my laptop and allow my mom and dad a glimpse into the unfolding of the day via Skype.

On this day, I was reminded by Scott that I needed to ask for help and be clear when I needed something, When I asked Jordan about doing that job, he took it on and did great. I am so proud of myself for stepping up and asking for what I needed. He gave my mom and dad the opportunity to be a part of my day, as they lived across the country in the littlest province in Canada—Prince Edward Island where I had grown up the first twenty-ish years of my life.

When it came to stepping up and asking for what I needed, I also asked Alannah to take pictures and videos. I knew she was a creative, thoughtful lady who would do a super job of capturing special moments in our day. About a year before our wedding and only a few months into my son dating Alannah, I had an incident at school where my heart was racing fast—an experience that I had never had before. I ended up being taken to the hospital in an ambulance, and my heartbeat settled down within a few hours. Tests concluded that there was no concern. In retrospect, it was probably all stress. This incident got back to Alannah. Later that evening, Jordan dropped off a homemade card and a bubble bath and Epsom salt from her. What an amazing gesture of love and care! I truly appreciated this loving gesture, and I knew she was a special girl for my awesome son from that day.

All the pieces were falling into place on this most momentous day. One area I worked diligently on during the ninety-day PLD was to not just wear a confidence costume but to *be confident*. On this special day, I needed to step up to the plate and just be confident. One area of my life that I know I continue to work on is my speaking ability. I did not want to read my vows from a paper. I wanted to feel my vows. However, I needed to make sure that all the special points I wanted to say would not be missed.

As Scott slipped away to get himself ready in his black tuxedo, white bow tie, his suspenders with the curse words in speech bubbles and, of course, those white Converse runners (sneakers is what we called them where I grew up), I took this time to review my vows. As I previously mentioned, I originally wrote my vows within a month or so of meeting Scott. I revamped them in January and then revamped them again in June.

VOWS - REWRITTEN IN JUNE

Scott, in the summer of 2021, I had finally met the man that was going to cherish me like I deserve and, babe, you show me that every single day.

When I first heard you speak (way back at the Ranch, 11 months ago), your heart was so open, so vulnerable.

You were so ready to be loved. It was at that point I knew your heart and my heart were meant to be together.

Babe, you have graciously held my heart with unconditional love and respect.

And I will forever hold your heart with honour and love.

*With you, Scott, I've found a love I
have never experienced before.*

A love so honest and so genuine.

A love I will never take for granted.

*I knew very early that you, Scott, were exactly what my heart
needed.*

We have balance.

We have an emotional connection.

We have desire.

*And we have a genuine love for each other to grow and to
become better people.*

*Scott, you are who I want to be with, grow old with, challenge
and enjoy life with.*

I love you now and forever.

You have forever changed my heart, and I thank you.

I want to be your wife, your soulmate and your partner in life.

*I love you, Scott Allen Brearley, and I am ready to be Mrs. Lisa
Dawn Brearley.*

It is interesting how I've discovered that words are so important to me. I want to be able to say them just right, or at least I want to make sure my message is clear. This is why I feel like my speaking ability (speaking eloquently from my PLD mantra) is so difficult for me. This is why I doubt my ability. I continue to work on this every day.

Over this past year, we've occasionally wondered if we were always enough for each other. Over the year, I often second-guessed myself in our relationship. Was I interesting enough? Was I adventurous enough to be with this man? As I learned to be more certain in my own skin, I learned I am enough. I bring love, patience, excitement, calmness and an appreciation for life to our relationship. These are things he appreciates about me.

He has shared that he sometimes feels like he is too much for me— too reactive, too damaged, too trauma-filled, too much of a risk-taker. I love that he is adventurous, takes on life with inspired interest, sees life as an endless chance for adventure and loves many things that I do!

By 4 p.m., our JP, Rene, had arrived as friends and family were all chipping in to organize things. Julie organized the table for signing the marriage licence, and friends were talking together. I was feeling the love in my house, that's for sure.

Rene was a kind-hearted soul, and I could instantly tell that she was going to be an integral part of making this a special day. Her calm, loving nature was perfect for our day. She, along with all our friends who attended, brought love and positivity. That's what we wanted. That's what we needed. That's what we manifested.

For my big entrance, I surprised Scott with a song (not the song that I had created for him). He had recently discovered a new artist, Jelly Roll—a rapper/country singer who, like Scott, has many stories of drinking and being down and out. Scott related to him, and there was one song that he and I really liked—"Save Me." While Scott connected with the words, he and I loved the flow of the song and Jelly Roll's voice and tone. So, I chose the acoustic version of this song. It was played for my grand entrance as I walked down the aisle.

Our wedding was planned in about three weeks. We knew it was an event where it wasn't about spending a lot of money on dresses or even location. We wanted our wedding to be simple. Earlier that week, I arranged the backyard patio into how I wanted it to look for this special day. I cut roses from my front yard and put them in wine glasses along my aisle and the patio area. We knew we wanted to enjoy and celebrate our love with our friends. That was our priority.

We had wonderful friends, neighbours and family join us on our day. The wedding party was lined up in chairs closer to the front, and neighbours and friends were standing on the grass.

It was also important to have my two amazing kids as part of this special day. At the same time, I did not want to scare them on their level of participation in the wedding ceremony. I was aware that this wedding might have been a little awkward for them, considering I had been with their father for twenty-six years, just separated a year before, left our family home and had just received the divorce papers a month before this special day. But I asked my kids to stand along the aisle, so I could hug them as I entered from the garage. Yes, I stood in the garage by myself and listened to the music, so I could start my walk up the 'aisle' (the sidewalk from our garage to the back patio) to Scott.

I came out of the garage, and I got to hug Brianna first. I told her I loved her and that I was so grateful she was there. I was filled with such joy that she got to experience how much this man loves and respects me.

Jordan stood beside Brianna, and I hugged him tightly. I told him I loved him. Having my two kids there on this day was a must. I was so filled with joy, happiness, love, and I was proud to have them celebrate with me on this joyous day.

Our ceremony was beautiful and was exactly what I was looking for. I asked for what I wanted and got it! Rene set the scene with love, peace and harmony. She highlighted that she appreciated how Scott and I genuinely cared for each other and that she felt fortunate to be part of this special day.

When it was time for our vows, I held Scott's hands, and I was first to speak.

"Do you remember what I said to you this morning? 'How can you love me today?'" I asked.

It was funny—at that moment, he could not recall. I reminded and guided him to look out at all the beautiful friends and family that were there and see how they all came because they love him and me. And then I started my vows.

I said most of the important points I wanted to get across and at one point drew a blank, something I would usually fret over and then totally go blank. However, this time (with some reassurance from Rene and Scott standing right in front of me), I continued to share my vows with Scott. I was proud of myself that day for speaking so eloquently.

As for Scott, I asked (later that day) how he remembered what he wanted to say. I asked, "Did you write it down?"

"No, I just said it off the top of my head," he answered.

Wow, a master of the speech for sure!

One very special part of Scott's vows was when he included my two children in it. He said that if anytime they need him (and he looked at them both), he was always there. And if anything should ever happen to me, he would be there. That truly took me by surprise. He truly is a man of beauty and a loving soul.

On our wedding day, we were surrounded with love from our family and friends. On this day, I got to marry my soulmate, Scott. A man who inspires me to complete myself, who loves me with so much conviction and so much heart that it is nearly impossible to doubt just how capable I am of becoming exactly who I have always wanted to be.

Thank you, Scott. I am so blessed to have found my soulmate.

Our wedding day on July 23, 2022

Acknowledgement

My life is better when I put the work in. When I take on challenges and risks. When I reach out for support. When I choose to grow my heart and my mind, and they expand for more opportunities. When I choose to be grateful for each and every day. When I step forward and live my life of liberty. When I know I am leaving a legacy. I continue to strive moving forward in my life as a confident woman, mother, wife and human being who can have a positive impact on this world.

I completed this book about eight months after my and Scott's wedding day while we were in Thailand for a six-month stay. Since I was on a leave from my full-time teaching job in Canada, I took this as an opportunity to complete this book and begin the sequel, called *Six Months of Love*.

In this sequel, I will take you on my journey of self-growth and the journey Scott and I have been on since we've been married. l will brief you on the time between our wedding and arriving in Thailand and then take you on a deeper dive of the journey of growth and love during our six-month stay in Thailand.

A huge acknowledgement and thank you to Natasa Denman, an award-winning author, speaker, coach, mentor and creator of the Ultimate 48 Hour Author system. Natasa has reminded me and all the authors she has worked with that "It's not about writing your first book; it's about the person you become at the other end of it."

She is so right. Thank you, Natasa.

About the Author

Lisa Brearley is a beautiful woman, partner, mother and teacher. She moved to the big city of Calgary, Alberta after marrying in 1995. For almost twenty years, she has been an elementary school teacher in the public system in Calgary. In 2019, she began to better herself through a program called Healthy Transformations, losing almost sixty pounds and gaining clarity in her thinking. With more bounce in her step, she took on several personal development programs and was starting to see the person she has become today.

After receiving her divorce papers in June 2022, she married the love of her life, Scott Brearley, on July 23, 2022. Together, they are exploring Thailand with open minds and hearts for new experiences. They are looking forward to more personal development with a year-long coaching course to spur their goals and desires in their lives filled with commitment and love for themselves and each other.

This is a snippet of her life from August 15, 2021 to July 23, 2022. A Year of Love and growth that she never knew was possible. Come join her on her journey of taking risks and expanding her mind and heart.

3 Offers With Calls to Action

1. Visit Lisa Brearley's website @ https://lgallant1973.wixsite.com/my-site-4 and click on 'Let's Chat' (with the subject heading BONUS PACK) and I will send you a FREE plan on improving your self-esteem *and* the link to our wedding song, "It All Pointed to You."

2. Book Lisa Brearley for a one-hour online presentation on her book, her personal growth journey and relationship reminders. As well, book Scott and Lisa for a two-hour presentation on their own personal growth journey and how they continue to see the benefit in how their own dedication to themselves supports their partnership. Visit Lisa's website for booking times: https://lgallant1973.wixsite.com/my-site-4

3. Visit Lisa's personal website to book her as your personal support to strengthen your self-esteem—the foundation of how you show up in life. Website: https://lgallant1973.wixsite.com/my-site-4

CPSIA information can be obtained
at www.ICGtesting.com
Printed in the USA
LVHW040425190523
747442LV00001B/4

9 781922 982063